Must-See Birds OF THE
PACIFIC NORTHWEST

Must-See Birds OF THE PACIFIC NORTHWEST

SARAH SWANSON AND MAX SMITH

TIMBER PRESS
Portland | London

Frontispiece: Pacific Wren

Photo credits appear on page 242.
Maps by Allison Berg

Published in 2013 by Timber Press, Inc.

The Haseltine Building
133 S.W. Second Avenue, Suite 450
Portland, Oregon 97204-3527
timberpress.com

6a Lonsdale Road
London NW6 6RD
timberpress.co.uk

Printed in China
Second printing 2014
Book design by Laken Wright

Library of Congress Cataloging-in-Publication Data

Swanson, Sarah, 1979–
 Must-see birds of the Pacific Northwest/Sarah Swanson and Max Smith.—1st ed.
   p. cm.
 Includes bibliographical references and index.
 ISBN 978-1-60469-337-9
 1. Birds—Northwest, Pacific. 2. Birds—Northwest, Pacific—Identification. 3. Bird
watching—Northwest,
Pacific. I. Smith, Max, 1978– II. Title.
 QL683.P16S93 2013
 598.072′34795—dc23   2013004183

TO OUR FAMILIES, FOR GIVING US CHILDHOODS FULL
OF EXPLORATION AND NATURE. WE LOVE YOU MORE THAN
PILEATED WOODPECKERS LOVE TO EAT ANTS.

Contents

Western Oregon and Washington

Introduction
BIRDING IN THE PACIFIC NORTHWEST

I n the Pacific Northwest, a seabird lays its egg in a nest on the mossy branch of an old-growth tree and flies out to the ocean each day in search of fish. Songbirds sing throughout the year, and tubenosed birds visit our shores from as far away as New Zealand. Even our largest cities attract spectacular flights of migratory birds. Birding hotspots include forested mountains, valley wetlands, Pacific shores, inland seas, and desert basins—enough to provide a lifetime of birding adventures.

The geographic boundaries of the Pacific Northwest vary widely depending on your purposes. This book is for people interested in birding opportunities unique to Oregon and Washington. For this reason, we include the portions of each state that contain types of natural areas that are unique to this part of the country. They include the Pacific Coast, the Salish Sea (Puget Sound and surrounding waters), the Willamette Valley and Puget Trough, the Cascade Range, and the eastern Cascade foothills. We do not include the easternmost portions of each state, because those areas include plant and bird communities that are characteristic of other regions such as the Rocky Mountains and the Great Basin.

We include several sites in Oregon and Washington where you're most likely to find interesting birds. We do not list sites for very common birds. These sites are not, by any means, the only places to find these birds in the Pacific Northwest. And we can't guarantee that the birds we mention will be present when you are, but that's part of what makes birding exciting. Most of these sites are specific, well-traveled locations such as parks, wildlife refuges, and waterways. Some locations require a parking or admission fee. A few are along rough roads, so always use discretion when it comes to road conditions and your vehicle's abilities.

This book introduces you to 85 of the Pacific Northwest's must-see birds and shares some remarkable information about their lives and must-visit places to find them. Although this book does not include all of the birds you'll see in the Pacific Northwest, we hope that it gives you the inspiration and information you need to go out and enjoy the many must-see birds of Oregon and Washington.

Essential Equipment

Birding is a wonderfully simple activity with only two critical steps: number one, find some birds, and number two, identify them. Here are some tips to help you succeed.

Binoculars and field guides are perhaps the only essential items for birding. The beginning birder will find a confusing array of options for both items. Binoculars, for example, range in price from less than $100 to more than $2000. When considering binoculars, you should test a few pairs by viewing objects close and distant to find which magnification (typically 8- or 10-power) works best for you. Ask the salesperson to help you figure out the eye adjustment, which is unique to each pair of eyes. Although no particular brand or price range is essential for bird sighting success in the Pacific Northwest, waterproof binoculars certainly are required.

Every birder has a favorite field guide, and a few own them all. One guide featuring all birds regularly found in North America (north of Mexico) is all you need to identify any bird you see in the Pacific Northwest and beyond. Such guides typically come in two forms: photographic or illustrated. For use in the field, we prefer illustrated guides, because each bird is placed in the position in which you are most likely to encounter it, and the artists are able to depict the features of each bird that are most helpful to identification. Books with photographs, such as ours, are helpful for getting to know birds before a birding trip or for confirming identification in concert with an illustrated guide.

A spotting scope is a helpful piece of equipment for identifying shorebirds, waterfowl, and seabirds at coastal and wetland sites, where your targets are a great distance away. If you have attended a field trip with a leader who provided a high-quality spotting scope, you know what a difference it makes. An all-weather notebook and pen or pencil are also useful for taking notes on a difficult-to-identify bird or for listing species found at a location so you can relocate them on a future visit.

The marine-influenced, temperate climate of western Oregon and Washington is conducive to year-round birding, provided you own waterproof binoculars, a rain jacket, and a pair of rubber boots. With so much to see here—so many fascinating birds that live in beautiful places—what are you doing inside? Grab your binoculars and go find some birds!

The Birds

All of our region's birds are appealing in some way, and it is difficult and somewhat arbitrary to assign must-see status to some but not others. However, we want to help you begin or expand your birding experience by steering you toward certain birds that are likely to spark your interest because they are eye-catching or unusual. In selecting species to include, we recalled the highlights of our own birding experiences and the birds that have excited people in the classes and walks that we've led. We hope you'll agree that all the birds we've included here are worth a look or a listen.

To make this book accessible to beginning and intermediate birders, we excluded some species that we find fascinating but that are too rare to find reliably, that are already familiar, or that are too challenging for most nonexperts to identify. These excluded birds include Gyrfalcons, American Robins, and the flycatchers of the genus *Empidonax*, respectively.

For each bird discussed in these pages, we provide one or more photos and list some field marks that are useful in identification. We describe the bird's calls and songs if they are helpful in locating and identifying it. We also share natural history facts in each bird's description, gleaned from recent ornithological literature. Finally, we tell you when and where you have the best chance of finding each species and provide a list of other birds to look for while you are there.

TAXONOMY AND JARGON

When discussing an individual species, most authorities provide both its genus and species names. This scientific name, such as *Haliaeetus leucocephalus*, is universal across all languages. The name most of us associate with a species, such as Bald Eagle, is the common name, which varies among languages. We provide both scientific and common names in our species accounts. We also refer to families of birds when necessary to discuss the commonalities within a group of related birds such as ducks or warblers.

Ornithologists and birders use group names to describe groups of birds based on their behavior and habitat use.

- Waterfowl are ducks, geese, and swans.
- Shorebirds are often found along the shores of oceans, lakes, and streams. They include sandpipers, plovers, and oystercatchers and display a variety of behaviors, including running along the sand, wading in shallow water, and probing muddy areas for food.
- Seabirds spend time on the open ocean and return to land to rest and nest. This group includes loons, grebes, murres, puffins, and albatrosses and their relatives.
- Wading birds include long-legged birds, most of which are larger than shorebirds, that step into water in search of fish and other aquatic prey. Well-known wading birds include herons, egrets, ibises, and storks.
- Land birds are not usually associated with water. This diverse group includes diurnal (active during the day) birds of prey (raptors, such as hawks and eagles), owls, woodpeckers, hummingbirds, and songbirds.

LOCATION AND IDENTIFICATION

Finding and identifying birds can be difficult when small birds are moving through dense vegetation. Be prepared to find birds using your eyes *and* ears. Move quietly and slowly, and keep conversation to a minimum. Even if you can't identify a bird by its song or call, listening for these sounds can alert you to its location so you can identify it by sight. When looking for small land birds, watch for movement. A flash of feathers or moving vegetation can betray the presence of a sneaky bird such as a warbler.

After you locate the bird, keep your eyes trained on it and lift your binoculars without looking down at them. It takes some practice, but a smooth transition from eyes to binoculars is essential to spotting birds on the move. Finding a bird while you're looking through your binoculars is much more difficult because your field of view is reduced.

Get a good look at a bird, make a note of what you see, and then use your field guide. Too often, we immediately pull out our field guides when confronted with a challenging identification. By the time we look up from the pages, the bird is gone and we wish we had spent more time looking at it. When you're viewing a mystery bird with others, quietly announce distinctive features such as colors, wing bars, or eye rings. When the bird is gone, recalling these field marks will help you all determine what you were looking at.

If you are having difficulty finding birds at an otherwise productive-looking site, pay attention to any species, even relatively common ones you have already seen. They may alert you to the presence of others, because multiple species often flock together, especially during the nonbreeding seasons.

After you've experienced finding and identifying some birds, your next steps are up to you: Compose a species list for your trip, your year, your yard, your county, and beyond; photograph your favorite birds; take part in birding trips; join birding groups such as the Audubon Society; and volunteer for surveys such as the Audubon Society's Christmas Bird Count or Cornell University's Project FeederWatch. When you have gained confidence and experience, you might even enjoy leading a bird walk of your own to share your knowledge with beginners. Sign up for electronic mailing lists, such as Oregon Birders Online (OBOL) for Oregon and Tweeters for Washington, and you can monitor bird sightings from around the region and share your discoveries.

Weekend Trips

We've provided eight ideas for weekend birding road trips: two-day excursions in central and western Oregon and Washington, where you can visit numerous sites and view a diversity of birds. We planned three trips for the winter months and five trips for the summer months based on birds you are likely to see during each season. If you take any of these trips during the spring or fall, you will likely see a mixture of winter and summer birds. Although there are no guarantees in birding, you do have a realistic chance of observing each must-see bird on at least one of the birding weekends, provided that you visit during the best time of the year.

Several productive stops are suggested for each weekend location. You'll find most of these on an up-to-date map or gazetteer. To help you select sites to visit, we list some of the must-see birds you are most likely to see at each stop, as well as several other interesting species you might see while you're there. Of course, you will probably see even more species than we list, so keep your field guide handy.

Birding Ethics

For the most part, birders are a gentle bunch who make a low impact on birds and other people. By following a simple code of ethics, you can protect birds and maintain goodwill toward birders everywhere. The American Birding Association code of ethics is a great standard and is available online at http://www.aba.org/about/ethics.html. We will highlight some of its points along with our own suggestions.

Place the well-being of birds ahead of your birding success. Birds must forage, care for young, migrate, and avoid predators. The margin of error for having enough energy to do it all is very thin. We believe it is important to limit the use of recorded songs or calls to lure birds into the open, although it is tempting to do so for you own convenience and gratification. However, you may be interrupting vital activities and compromising an individual's survival, especially in heavily birded locations or during the breeding season.

Respect private property, landowner rules, and regulations. With the tourism dollars they bring, birders are welcomed to many areas in our region and we would like to keep it that way. Avoid trespassing at all times, and don't block public roadways or private driveways. Unless you've asked for permission, it is probably a bad idea to view a private residence or its bird feeders with binoculars.

Male
Wood Duck

THE
BIRDS

Heermann's Gull

Beach Birds

DENIZENS OF THE WAVES, ROCKS, AND SAND

THE NORTHWEST COAST attracts not only human tourists but also many avian visitors. Birds from a variety of families float in the water, run along the sand, and try to steal a meal at the beach. The beach can include the land along the Pacific Ocean, coastal bays and rivers, and the Salish Sea, a large system of saltwater bodies in northwest Washington that includes Puget Sound. You'll find beach birds in these areas throughout the year. Other birds travel here from the north, south, east, and west to spend their summers or winters, taking advantage of the mild climate and abundant oceanic food.

Many diverse birds make their homes at the beach. Ducks, cormorants, shorebirds, and gulls are commonly recognized groups, but alcids are a little more obscure. The alcids are a coastal family of penguinlike birds that are awkward on land but can fly both in the air and under water. The family includes puffins, auklets, murres, murrelets, guillemots, and the flightless Great Auk, which is extinct.

Tufted Puffins

HARLEQUIN DUCK

Histrionicus histrionicus

NO OTHER DUCK in our region has the fortitude to raise its young in a rushing stream and then spend the winter in a storm-tossed sea. As if this behavior weren't enough to impress, male Harlequin Ducks possess stunningly brilliant plumage, with white patches that illuminate the grayest of coastal days. The more subdued female resembles a polished rock as she wades in rushing water.

Slate-blue plumage with chestnut patches and bold white stripes make the male Harlequin Duck instantly recognizable. The drab female is more likely to blend in with the rocks, but her white facial spots give her away. Harlequins have a rounded appearance with a very short neck and stubby bill. Other coastal ducks with white spots include Buffleheads and Surf Scoters, but the male Bufflehead has larger

Male
Harlequin
Ducks

white patches than the Harlequin and the female is tiny with a single white spot. Surf Scoters are larger and chunkier than Harlequins with longer, heavier bills.

FOOD AND FORAGING

Harlequin Ducks are devoted consumers of aquatic invertebrates—caddisfly larvae in mountain streams are a large component of their summer diets. Crabs, barnacles, and snails are on the menu during coastal winters, and they will occasionally eat fish and fish eggs as well. During a typical 30-second dive below the water's surface, a Harlequin picks prey from submerged rocks or the ocean floor and may disturb the floor with its feet to stir up prey.

PAIRING AND PARENTING

Harlequins are among the few ducks that maintain pair bonds from year to year, although the female performs the nesting duties on her own. She places her nest near a mountain stream on an island of sorts—on a heap of woody debris, on top of a stump, in a large tree cavity, on a cliff above the stream, or under a dense tangle of shrubs. She incubates an average of five eggs

for 30 days and then leads her newly hatched young to a stream, where they immediately exhibit their swimming and insect-catching prowess. After 50 days, when the young are capable of flight, the family migrates to the coast and the parents reunite. Juvenile females may spend the winter with their parents, but young males disperse to find their own wintering sites.

MIGRATIONS AND MOVEMENTS

Harlequins migrate in an east-west pattern. Nonbreeding birds remain at the coast year-round, but breeding birds fly inland beginning in March to nest along mountain streams. During the summer, males gather at sites such as the Oregon Coast and the Salish Sea while the females are incubating their eggs. Females return to the coast and occupy their wintering areas by the end of October.

WHERE TO FIND HARLEQUIN DUCKS

Because they purposely choose inaccessible streams for nesting, Harlequins are best spotted during nonbreeding times at the coast. Scan

rocky areas near shore for the frequently diving ducks. They also perch on rocks and climb onto floating mats of kelp.

In Washington

Marlyn Nelson County Park near Sequim

Fort Worden State Park near Port Townsend

Fort Flagler State Park near Port Townsend

Cattle Point on San Juan Island

In Oregon

Haystack Rock in Cannon Beach

Seal Rock State Wayside near Newport

Cape Arago State Park near Coos Bay

Eagle Creek in the Columbia Gorge (nesting)

OTHER BIRDS TO SEE

Bays and inlets with rocky bottoms are excellent foraging sites for winter waterfowl and seabirds. Look for Common Goldeneyes, SURF SCOTERS, RED-BREASTED MERGANSERS, PIGEON GUILLEMOTS, Red-throated Loons, and many other actively feeding birds.

Female
Harlequin
Duck

SURF SCOTER

Melanitta perspicillata

SURF SCOTERS ARE gregarious ducks with a clownlike appearance. Found almost everywhere on the Northwest Coast during winter, it would be an easy bird to take for granted, but its comically large bill and odd facial plumage make it worth a look every time. Surf Scoters gather in huge floating groups, or rafts, and they all disappear as they dive below the surface in unison.

Built for riding ocean waves, these ducks are sturdy. The males are black with attention-getting white patterns on their heads and colorful beaks; females are a more subtle dark brown with whitish patches on their face. To tell them apart from other scoters, look for the large white patch on the back of the head—it's brighter on the male, but the female has it, too. The male's forehead also has a white patch.

FOOD AND FORAGING

In the winter, Surf Scoters are primarily bivalve hunters, diving under the surface to capture clams and mussels. During the nesting season, they transition to a diverse freshwater diet of aquatic insects, crustaceans, worms, and freshwater mussels. During springtime migration, northbound Surf Scoters visit herring spawning grounds to fill up on caviar.

PAIRING AND PARENTING

Forgive the female Surf Scoter if she seems quite careless with her young. After arriving with a mate at a lakeside nest site, she lays six to nine eggs, and then the male departs. When the eggs hatch 30 days later, she leads her brood to the water, where they often mix with other Surf Scoter young, forming multifamily broods tended by multiple females. Adult females leave the nesting grounds before the young are capable of flight. The abandoned ducklings form a group and later migrate to the coast.

MIGRATIONS AND MOVEMENTS

Although Surf Scoters do not nest in Oregon or Washington, you can see nonbreeding individuals in the Pacific Ocean and the Salish Sea throughout the year. Breeding birds leave the Northwest to nest in Canada and Alaska by the end of May. These birds begin returning to our area in July, but some may not arrive until November.

WHERE TO FIND SURF SCOTERS

Surf Scoters are common sights at the coast, riding breaking waves in the ocean or in a sheltered bay. You can see a few of these attention-getting birds from just about anywhere with a good view of the water. They are found often in large flocks, making them easy to spot. They might be resting in deep water or diving for food near a jetty or pier.

OTHER BIRDS TO SEE

Jetties provide excellent vantage points for watching birds such as Black Scoters, COMMON LOONS, Red-necked Grebes, and Pelagic Cormorants in the winter. These areas also host rock-loving shorebirds such as BLACK TURNSTONES and Surfbirds. Don't go out too far onto the jetty; winter seas can push large waves over the top without notice.

Male Surf
Scoter

Female
Surf Scoter

LONG-TAILED DUCK

Clangula hyemalis

THE LONG-TAILED DUCK exchanged its former name, Oldsquaw, for a perfectly descriptive name, although it doesn't apply to the short-tailed females. Its showy, multicolored plumage sets it apart from other wintering ducks, and its comparative rarity makes it an exciting bird to find. A sighting of this small duck leaves a big impression.

Two slim tail feathers extend about 12 inches behind the male, giving the species its name. Females lack long tail plumes, but they share the pied (splotched) black, brown, and white coloration of the males. Long-tailed Ducks are too small to be mistaken for snow geese or swans, so identifying them is simple. Scoters are also black-and-white sea ducks, but they are darker overall. Pintails have somewhat long tails, but they have dark heads and are graceful and long-necked. Pigeon Guillemots are also predominantly white in the winter, but they are smaller and lack any brown coloration.

FOOD AND FORAGING

This sea duck prefers calmer, deeper water than its coastal compatriots the Surf Scoter and Harlequin Duck. It plunges nearly 200 feet below the surface in search of invertebrates, fish eggs, and aquatic plants. Long-taileds will occasionally chase down and consume fish, but crustaceans such as shrimp and isopods make up the bulk of their diet.

PAIRING AND PARENTING

Males and females pair on wintering grounds and travel together to nesting sites on the shores of arctic lakes. The female adds her own down feathers to a shallow depression in the soil of an island or a peninsula while laying up to eight eggs. Young hatch after a 26-day incubation period and follow the female to water. They can find their own food at the surface but do not begin diving until they have grown larger. Juvenile Long-tailed Ducks grow quite rapidly compared to other ducklings and are capable of flight 35 to 40 days after hatching, just in time to flee an early arctic winter.

MIGRATIONS AND MOVEMENTS

After the nesting season, Long-tailed Ducks begin arriving at the Northwest Coast in October and stay until May, when they depart again for their arctic nesting grounds. The majority of the West Coast population spends the winter on the coasts of Alaska and British Columbia. Lucky for us, a few venture down to northwest Washington. Fewer still visit coastal Oregon.

WHERE TO FIND LONG-TAILED DUCKS

This species is much more common in Washington and always noteworthy in Oregon. Look for them in the Salish Sea or in large bays on the Oregon Coast. They might be in the company of scoters or other diving birds. Their whiteness makes them stand out from nearby scoters and mergansers.

In Washington

Dungeness National Wildlife Refuge near Sequim

Marlyn Nelson County Park near Sequim

Fort Flagler State Park near Port Townsend

Samish Island near Anacortes

In Oregon

Coos Bay

Yaquina Bay near Newport

Siuslaw River, South Jetty, near Florence

OTHER BIRDS TO SEE

Long-tailed Ducks are often found floating in groups with other wintering water birds. Check the area for SURF SCOTERS, White-winged Scoters, COMMON LOONS, BRANT, RUDDY DUCKS, and Horned Grebes.

RED-BREASTED MERGANSER

Mergus serrator

Male Red-breasted Merganser

DON'T JUDGE A duck by its punk rock hairstyle. Red-breasted Mergansers don't have a bad attitude; they are actually quite sedate as they cruise through the tidewater in search of fish. The sharp spikiness of their head feathers and toothiness of their orange, serrated bills give them a more reptilian look than other ducks, but small, aquatic creatures are the only ones that have anything to fear.

This bird makes a big impression. The male is especially eye-catching, with a patchwork of black, gray, white, brown, and green feathers in addition to his bright bill and crazy hairstyle. The only bird that shares the distinctive bill is the Common Merganser, but clear differences exist between the two. The spiky crest and dark cinnamon chest on the male Red-breasted is very different from the smooth head and white chest of the male Common Merganser. Females are a little more challenging to tell apart. The Red-breasted's crest is spiky, while

the Common's is shaggy. The Common Merganser female displays a crisp contrast between its gray body, rusty head, and bright white chin, while the female Red-breasted's colors blend into each other more smoothly.

FOOD AND FORAGING

Like other mergansers, Red-breasteds use their serrated bills to keep a tight grip on fish, shrimp, aquatic insects, worms, and amphibians while diving below the surface. These divers have a wide repertoire of underwater foraging techniques, including fish chasing, collaborative herding, and crevice probing.

PAIRING AND PARENTING

After pairs arrive on their tundra or boreal forest nesting grounds, the female selects a nest site on the ground within 75 feet of a body of water. She incubates ten eggs for 30 days. Typical of ducks, the male leaves before the ducklings hatch. Females sometimes abandon their young, leaving them in the care of other hens. Adult females leave the rearing area before the youngsters are capable of flight. At 60 days after hatching, the ducklings can fly and soon migrate to coastal wintering sites.

MIGRATIONS AND MOVEMENTS

Red-breasted Mergansers spend the winter in coastal areas and migrate to their northern nesting sites in spring. Most birds leave the Northwest by the end of May and arrive at their nesting grounds in June. Wintering birds return to Oregon and Washington from September to November.

WHERE TO FIND RED-BREASTED MERGANSERS

This species is rarely found away from saltwater but seems to prefer protected bays. They are easy to find, but that doesn't make them any less enjoyable. Just scan the water of bays and river mouths for their spiky silhouettes.

In Washington

Alki Beach in West Seattle

Point Brown Jetty in Ocean Shores

Elwha River mouth

John Wayne Marina near Sequim

In Oregon

Netarts Bay near Netarts

Bayocean Spit on Tillamook Bay

South Jetty of the Coquille River near Bandon

Yaquina Bay near Newport

OTHER BIRDS TO SEE

Mergansers diving for fish in bays during the winter have plenty of company and competition from WESTERN GREBES, COMMON LOONS, Red-necked Grebes, BRANDT'S CORMORANTS, and COMMON MURRES.

Female
Red-breasted
Merganser

COMMON LOON

Gavia immer

THE COMMON LOON has a reputation for being a loud, sharply adorned pond dweller. During winters at the coast, however, this loon adopts a more subdued persona, quietly blending with its gray surroundings, and swimming and diving to feed its voracious appetite for fish and crabs.

You'll often see Common Loons on the Pacific Coast in their drab winter plumage— dark gray above and white below and on their chin. In the spring, you might see one transitioning to the famous iridescent black head, bill, and throat stripes they sport during the breeding season. The Common Loon's large, bayonetlike bill is thicker than those of Pacific and Red-throated Loons. Weighing in at nine

pounds, the Common Loon is one of the biggest, heaviest birds found in winter seas. Yellow-billed Loons are even larger but much rarer.

FOOD AND FORAGING

While floating at the surface, Common Loons often poke their head into the water like a snorkeling human to look for fish. Under water, they propel themselves by kicking their webbed feet simultaneously. They capture prey in their spearlike bill and swallow smaller fish and crabs while still under water. Larger prey is brought to the surface if the bird needs some time to swallow it.

PAIRING AND PARENTING

Birds remain paired for several years but are together only during the nesting season. After arriving independently at the nesting grounds, the male and female begin constructing a nest on the shore of a lake or pond. The female lays

Common Loon, breeding plumage

one or two eggs, and both parents incubate them for 28 days. Like ducklings, loon chicks can leave the nest the day they hatch and swim with their parents. Unlike ducklings, loon chicks do not capture their own food, relying on parents to bring them fish or other aquatic animals. In one of nature's cutest sights, a chick will frequently catch a ride on a parent's back while the other parent feeds it fish. Eleven weeks after hatching, chicks can capture all of their own food, and a week later, they can fly.

MIGRATIONS AND MOVEMENTS

In late summer or early fall, Common Loons arrive on the coast from their nesting grounds on freshwater lakes and slow-moving rivers throughout the northern United States and Canada. In April and May, adults transition to their snappy breeding plumage and then depart for their inland nesting grounds. Some immature birds, which resemble wintering adults, are present along the Pacific Coast and in the Salish Sea throughout the summer.

WHERE TO FIND COMMON LOONS

Common Loon, winter plumage

Widespread and fairly abundant in winter, Common Loons frequent all coastal waters.

Watch for them floating, diving, and snorkeling in salt water and fresh water. They are usually the biggest seabird out there, making them easy to spot.

In Washington

Padilla Bay near Burlington

Westport fishing pier observation point

Willapa Bay near Long Beach

Utsalady Bay on Camano Island

Potlatch State Park on Hood Canal

In Oregon

Yaquina Bay near Newport

Tillamook Bay near Tillamook

Columbia River, South Jetty, in Fort Stevens State Park, near Astoria

Columbia River from Marine Drive in Portland

OTHER BIRDS TO SEE

The rich eelgrass beds and shallow waters in places such as Padilla Bay are great locales for seeing American Wigeons, EURASIAN WIGEONS, BRANT, BALD EAGLES, BELTED KINGFISHERS, and GREAT BLUE HERONS.

BRANDT'S CORMORANT

Phalacrocorax penicillatus

Brandt's Cormorant, breeding plumage

DURING COURTSHIP RITUALS, Brandt's Cormorants strike yogalike poses to show off their brilliant blue throat pouches. All that yoga hasn't mellowed them out, though—they can still be cranky and aggressive when their nests are threatened, and other birds seek their protection as neighbors. These sociable swimmers do not fear the open ocean; they can dive to depths of more than 150 feet deep in waters hundreds of feet off the coast.

You might find it confusing to differentiate among the three cormorant species found on the West Coast, but a close look will reveal some helpful field marks. All three are blackish with long, snaky necks and long bills. Both the Brandt's and Double-crested are larger than the slim Pelagic. In breeding season, Brandt's have a blue throat patch, buff-colored chin feathers, and white plumes on their cheeks. Double-crested Cormorants fly with a kinked neck and have a large patch of orange skin on their face. Pelagic Cormorants are easy to discern in the early summer, when they sport a white patch on each side, between the wing and the tail.

FOOD AND FORAGING

Brandt's Cormorants patrol rocky reefs, swaying kelp forests, and muddy ocean bottoms for fish and squid. All cormorants propel themselves under water by kicking their feet while holding their wings tightly against their bodies. They pursue single fish or schools of fish, capturing them in their hooked bills. Brandt's often forage in groups, sometimes joining feeding frenzies of other bird species, and they will even hunt alongside sea lions.

PAIRING AND PARENTING

Upon arrival at cliff and island nesting sites, males begin constructing nests and performing displays to catch the attention of females. In one display, he tilts his head backward, nearly resting it on his back; holds up his wings at an odd angle; and cocks his tail. This display highlights his electric blue throat pouch and white whiskerlike cheek plumes. Males also fly around a nest colony with large wads of green nesting material tucked into their bills. If a female is impressed, the two hold the material in their bills together and use it to complete the drum-shaped nest. The female lays two to five eggs, and both parents incubate for 30 days. Nestlings resemble black baby dragons and stick their entire heads into the throats of their parents at feeding time, which ensures that they do not miss a drop of partially digested fish.

MIGRATIONS AND MOVEMENTS

Brandt's spend their entire lives on or near the Pacific Coast of North America. Post-breeding movements are dictated by fish availability, which changes in response to ocean conditions. Many birds disperse from the Northwest after the nesting season, so they may be more difficult to find in winter than in summer. Breeding birds begin returning to their coastal nesting sites in April or May.

WHERE TO FIND BRANDT'S CORMORANTS

Most of the listed sites are breeding locations where you can see this species in all its blue-throated glory. The birds are scattered around the coast during winter but are still present. When swimming, Brandt's travel in groups and ride low in the water with their bodies barely visible. They perch on rocks and spread their wings to dry in between fishing excursions. At breeding sites, they build their nests on a rock or cliff side.

In Washington

Cape Disappointment State Park near Ilwaco

Commencement Bay near Tacoma (winter)

Fort Worden State Park near Port Townsend

San Juan Islands Ferry (not during nesting time)

In Oregon

Yaquina Head Outstanding Natural Area near Newport

Barview Jetty at Tillamook Bay

Coquille Point in Bandon

Harris Beach State Park near Brookings

OTHER BIRDS TO SEE

During the nesting season, offshore rocks are covered with birds such as Pelagic Cormorants, PIGEON GUILLEMOTS, COMMON MURRES, TUFTED PUFFINS, BLACK OYSTERCATCHERS, and Western Gulls.

BLACK OYSTERCATCHER

Haematopus bachmani

WITH ITS UNMISTAKABLE orange bill and piercing call, the Black Oystercatcher is easy to detect and identify. This bird has charisma to spare and is always fun to watch as it goes about its noisy business. The coast offers a myriad of gulls, an abundance of alcids (such as puffins), and scores of sandpipers, but the flashy Black Oystercatcher is truly one-of-a-kind.

With its woodpeckerlike orange bill, chickenlike pink legs, and crowlike body, this bird looks as though it were assembled from spare parts. If you can get a close look at one through binoculars or a spotting scope, check out the orange ring around its yellow eye. This is the only dark bird with a bright orange bill and pink legs that you will find at the beach.

FOOD AND FORAGING

Black Oystercatchers use their chisel-shaped bills to jab mussels free from their shells, pry limpets off rocks, and pull crabs from their hiding places. Their diet includes a variety of marine invertebrates but, despite their name, few oysters. Their strong, fleshy feet help them grip wave-swept rocks while searching for food at low tide.

PAIRING AND PARENTING

This species lives life on the edge—even while nesting. When visiting rocky shorelines, you might see Black Oystercatchers sitting on nests that appear dangerously close to the surf. No need to worry—the eggs can still hatch even after being submerged during high tides. The incubation period lasts 26 to 28 days. The one to three chicks are precocial, meaning that they leave the nest and find their own food within days of hatching. They aren't abandoned by their parents, however; parents care for young for months after they leave the nest. It takes a long time to master the art of mussel-jabbing.

MIGRATIONS AND MOVEMENTS

During the nesting season, adults vociferously defend their foraging and nesting territories from other oystercatchers. Nesting usually takes place during the months of May and June. As winter approaches, some adults join younger birds to form small wintering flocks that roam the coastlines until it is time to nest again.

WHERE TO FIND BLACK OYSTERCATCHERS

Look for Black Oystercatchers at rocky coastal sites across the region. You'll see them on rocks near the shore or from lookout points on capes and headlands. Plan to go birding during a mid-to-low tide to watch them actively feeding. Rocky areas with exposed mussel beds are always a good bet. Throughout the year, listen for their loud, whistled calls often made during flight. During the breeding season, scan exposed rocky areas for the telltale orange bill of an incubating adult.

In Washington

San Juan County Park on San Juan Island

Rosario Beach near Anacortes

Fort Flagler State Park near Port Townsend

John Wayne Marina near Sequim

In Oregon

Haystack Rock near Cannon Beach

Cape Meares State Park near Tillamook

Yaquina Head Outstanding Natural Area near Newport

Many state parks and waysides south of Newport

OTHER BIRDS TO SEE

Other birds of interest near the rocky shore include Pelagic Cormorants nesting on tall rocks and cliffs, Surfbirds and BLACK TURN-STONES flying from rock to rock, and HARLE-QUIN DUCKS, SURF SCOTERS, and PIGEON GUILLEMOTS floating in the waves. Check out the bright-green giant anemones, orange and purple sea stars, and intricately patterned limpets in the tide pools.

BLACK TURNSTONE

Arenaria melanocephala

THESE BUSY, SOCIAL shorebirds constantly chatter to their flock mates as they pick through the seaweed-covered rocks. Perhaps they're chastising one another for stealing the tastiest snails. These birds' comical and endearing behavior, extreme loyalty to wintering sites, and ease of identification make them great introductory shorebirds. Identifying a Black Turnstone is not nearly as confusing as sorting out those little brownish sandpipers known collectively as peeps.

Larger than peeps, but smaller than oystercatchers, these round-bodied, short-billed shorebirds have beautiful plumage that blends in well with wet rocks. When a Peregrine Falcon flies over, Black Turnstones duck down to look like cobbles. During the winter, the all-black head, black-and-white wings, and white belly are unique. In flight, white stripes on the wings, tail, and body are revealed. Their close relatives, Ruddy Turnstones, have similar patterns but are extremely rare in the Northwest. Black Turnstones are often found in the company of gray Surfbirds with yellow beaks.

FOOD AND FORAGING

As their name indicates, these midsized shorebirds will flip rocks to find edible morsels, although they spend much of their time investigating washed up fronds of seaweed and eelgrass. The flexible foragers also scrape limpets and barnacles off rocks, probe the sand for tiny animals, and even pick up birdseed off the ground near beachfront bird feeders.

PAIRING AND PARENTING

Males arrive first at nesting grounds in coastal Alaska and begin scraping depressions in the ground for a nest. Females eventually join the males, and they work in pairs to complete their nests by adding bits of vegetation to the scrape. The female lays four eggs, and both parents incubate them for 22 days. A few hours after hatching, the parents lead their chicks to buggy areas where they capture insects on their own. Young can fly about 35 days after hatching. Parents depart the nesting grounds at this time, and the young migrate to wintering sites several weeks later.

MIGRATIONS AND MOVEMENTS

The nesting range of this species is limited to the Alaskan coast, but the winter range stretches from southern Alaska to northwestern Mexico. Despite the distance between their nesting grounds and their wintering areas in Oregon and Washington, Black Turnstones spend very little time away from our region. Arrival at coastal wintering sites begins in July, and many birds do not leave for the nesting season until the following May.

WHERE TO FIND BLACK TURNSTONES

These birds forage where low tide reveals algae-covered rocks. If it's low tide and the birds are busy turning stones, you'll probably hear them

chattering back and forth before you see them. Scan the rocks at jetties, watching for their constant movement. During high tide, you might walk right by a bunch of black rocks that are actually Black Turnstones resting on high ground.

In Washington

Ediz Hook near Port Angeles

Point Brown Jetty near Ocean Shores

Penn Cove on Whidbey Island

Alki Beach in West Seattle

In Oregon

Rocky beach near Pacific Oyster Company store and restaurant in Bay City

Nehalem Bay State Park boat launch near Nehalem

Seaside Cove in Seaside

Mouth of Depoe Bay

Bandon Boat Basin inlet in Bandon

OTHER BIRDS TO SEE

Rocky shores could also hold Surfbirds, SURF SCOTERS, BLACK OYSTERCATCHERS, GREAT BLUE HERONS, and possibly a rare Rock Sandpiper.

RED-NECKED PHALAROPE

Phalaropus lobatus

Female
Red-necked
Phalarope,
breeding
plumage

SPENDING ITS WINTERS adrift on stormy seas, this delicate bird gathers tiny bits of food from the surface of the water. Females are bigger with brighter plumage than the males, and when nesting time arrives, the males stay at home with the kids.

Phalaropes are the only Northwest shorebird you are likely to see swimming; other shorebirds will be wading in shallow water or walking on land. Red-necked Phalaropes have skinny necks, small heads, and thin beaks, giving them a delicate appearance. They often spin in place to stir up aquatic food. Their non-breeding, winter plumage is gray, and in breeding plumage, the females display a white throat, red neck, and black mask. Males are drabber and lack the bright red on the neck. The Red-necked is the only one of our three phalarope species likely to be found along the coast during spring migration. Wilson's Phalaropes populate inland lakes and Red Phalaropes are far out to sea.

FOOD AND FORAGING

Phalaropes spend much of their time swimming, pecking at prey on or near the surface. During the winter, Red-necked Phalaropes concentrate their foraging efforts in areas high in plankton on the open ocean. During migration, they also forage in bays, ponds, and sewage lagoons. In the breeding season, they search for aquatic insects in lakes or small ponds. Like other phalaropes, they exhibit a circular swimming behavior, spinning like a top to whirl bits of food to the water's surface, where it can be picked up easily.

PAIRING AND PARENTING

All phalaropes display a serious reversal of the avian norm in parental roles. In breeding season, females are more brightly colored than males, have higher testosterone levels, and may mate with several males. Females lay four eggs in a nest and leave the male to incubate them on his own for 20 days. The male leads the chicks to areas where they can catch their own insects by walking or swimming. Young can fly by the time they are 20 days old and depart the nesting area after the adult males, eventually joining flocks of adults at wintering grounds.

MIGRATIONS AND MOVEMENTS

Red-necked Phalaropes breed across the arctic tundra and winter at sea. During spring migration, from April to June, however, you can see many individuals in the bays and sewage lagoons of the Pacific Northwest. During their southbound fall migration, from July to September, Red-necked Phalaropes mix with Wilson's Phalaropes in large flocks on lakes and ponds in eastern Oregon and Washington, taking advantage of abundant aquatic insect emergences. Flocks can be seen in the fall along the coast as well, but in smaller numbers.

WHERE TO FIND RED-NECKED PHALAROPES

Red-necked Phalarope, transitioning into winter plumage

This is one beach bird that also shows up inland, especially on lakes and at sewage treatment ponds. They are almost always found on the water, usually in small flocks. Their busy twirling movements are sure to catch your attention.

In Washington

Point Brown and Westport jetties near Grays Harbor

Hoquiam Sewage Treatment Plant near Hoquiam (check in at the office)

Port Angeles to Victoria ferry (in the air and on the water)

Crockett Lake on Whidbey Island

In Oregon

Nehalem Bay Sewage Ponds near Nehalem (only in designated areas)

Fernhill Wetlands in Forest Grove

Yaquina Bay and jetty area near Newport

Columbia River, South Jetty, in Fort Stevens State Park near Astoria

OTHER BIRDS TO SEE

Sewage treatment plant lagoons can be excellent birding sites, if you don't mind a bit of an odor. During spring migration, you might see Northern Shovelers, Ring-necked Ducks, RUDDY DUCKS, WOOD DUCKS, many species of swallows, and gulls. A PEREGRINE FALCON or BALD EAGLE might stop by to stir things up. Many sewage treatment plants happily allow birders but ask that you check in first and stay within designated areas.

BONAPARTE'S GULL

Chroicocephalus philadelphia

Bonaparte's
Gull, winter
plumage

THE BONAPARTE'S GULL did not seem to get the memo that it is actually a gull. Delicate and quiet, it distinguishes itself from larger gulls by nesting in trees. It also sports a black head during the breeding season and actively forages for aquatic prey in a ternlike manner. It scampers along the shoreline like a shorebird and spins in the water like a phalarope. With its large repertoire of interesting behaviors, the Bonaparte's is truly a Renaissance bird.

This gull is small with a buoyant flight style similar to that of a tern. The combination of a black spot behind the eye in winter plumage and a thin, black bill differentiates it from all other gulls in the region. It sports a black hood in breeding plumage, as does the red-billed and black-legged Franklin's Gull, but the Bonaparte's pink legs and black bill are unmistakable.

FOOD AND FORAGING

This small gull captures small prey, including tiny fish, fish eggs, krill, and insects. Larger gulls follow humans, waiting for a handout, but Bonaparte's Gulls search for food in a variety of watery habitats, appearing to work much harder than the other gulls. Bonaparte's hunt by plunging into water, dipping their bills into the water while flying, or picking at prey while floating on the surface. They sometimes spin in circles to whirl prey to the surface like a phalarope.

PAIRING AND PARENTING

Most gull species nest on the ground or on rocks in colonies, but Bonaparte's pairs nest singly or in small groups and construct most of their nests in coniferous trees in soggy boreal forests across Canada and Alaska. The male and female work together to build the nest, and both incubate the two or three eggs during the 24-day incubation period. Chicks spend a very short time in the nest, leaping from their tree 2 to 7 days after hatching. Like waterfowl, Bonaparte's parents lead the young to water, where they will swim and follow their parents until they can fly.

MIGRATIONS AND MOVEMENTS

Large flocks of Bonaparte's wander the coasts of Oregon and Washington in the winter to take advantage of changing food sources. Adults depart the Pacific Northwest for nesting grounds by the end of May, but one-year-old birds, too young to nest, may stick around during the summer months. Post-breeding migrants begin arriving from their northern nesting grounds in July or August.

WHERE TO FIND BONAPARTE'S GULLS

You'll find flocks of Bonaparte's Gulls gathered along the Salish Sea and the Oregon and Washington coasts in the fall, winter, and spring. They also show up at inland lakes and ponds. Look for small, light-colored gulls that fly like swallows with lots of swooping and plunging. In calm water, they might be floating on the surface.

In Washington

Fort Worden State Park near Port Townsend

Point No Point Lighthouse and County Park near Kingston

Discovery Park, West Point, in Seattle

Everett Sewage Ponds near Everett (register at the office)

Crescent Beach in Eastsound on Orcas Island

In Oregon

Netarts Bay near Netarts

Columbia River, South Jetty, in Fort Stevens State Park near Astoria

Boiler Bay State Scenic Viewpoint near Depoe Bay

Fernhill Wetlands near Forest Grove

OTHER BIRDS TO SEE

While you're enjoying the bonanza of Bonaparte's Gulls, look for HARLEQUIN DUCKS, White-winged Scoters, Red-necked Grebes, Horned Grebes, Pelagic Cormorants, and PIGEON GUILLEMOTS.

Bonaparte's Gull, breeding plumage

HEERMANN'S GULL

Larus heermanni

A UNIQUE GULL that breeds on a group of islands off the coast of western Mexico, Heermann's migrate northward after nesting, all the while tormenting their perennial companion, the Brown Pelican. In fact, the Heermann's Gull makes a living stalking pelicans and harassing them to share the larger birds' catch of fish. You know it's summer when you see a line of pelicans flying across the water, each escorted by a relentless, red-billed shadow.

This striking gull, with its distinctive orange-red bill, won't give you a field guide headache—that is, you won't spend time looking back and forth at nearly identical yellow-billed gull images while trying to identify a Heermann's perched on a rock. The Heermann's adult plumage, just as exceptional as its bill, features an unstreaked gray belly like no other gull in the area, dark gray wings, and a clean white head. Other immature Northwest gulls have brownish plumage, while the Heermann's plumage is dark gray.

FOOD AND FORAGING

The Heermann's Gull swims and plunges for fish and plucks them from the ocean while flying. Serious kleptoparasites (food thieves), their preferred mark is the Brown Pelican. It is common to see a flock of Brown Pelicans flying by, each pursued by a Heermann's Gull, hoping to steal fish when the pelican surfaces after a successful dive.

PAIRING AND PARENTING

Nearly the entire population of nesting Heermann's Gulls resides on one island in the northern Gulf of California, with the rest scattered among 10 to 20 rocky desert islands off the coast of western Mexico. Pairs build nests on the rocks or in grass, surrounded by dozens of other nesting birds. Both parents incubate one or two eggs for 28 days. During the nestling period, parents return to the noisy colony to find their chicks and regurgitate a meal. The dark gray young can fly at 45 days but do not attempt to nest until they have grown adult plumage, when they are three or four years old.

MIGRATIONS AND MOVEMENTS

This species has a rather unusual period of occurrence on the Northwest Coast. Flocks arrive in late June and depart the region by the middle of November. Heermann's Gulls begin nesting at their island colonies in early spring, and when the nesting season is over, they migrate to the Pacific Northwest.

WHERE TO FIND HEERMANN'S GULLS

Look for Heermann's Gulls close to the ocean or in the lower parts of estuaries. They might be flying over the beach or resting on a jetty or mudflat. Check flocks of pelicans for smaller gray companions. Also check congregations of gulls, because they sometimes mix with other species.

In Washington

Cape Disappointment State Park near Ilwaco

Edmonds Pier in Edmonds

Ocean City State Park beach access near Ocean Shores

Keystone Harbor on Whidbey Island

In Oregon

Columbia River, South Jetty, in Fort Stevens State Park near Astoria

Necanicum Estuary Park in Seaside

Siuslaw River, South Jetty, near Florence

Lone Ranch State Wayside near Brookings

OTHER BIRDS TO SEE

Keep your eyes open when you take a walk along the beach; you might get a flyover from BROWN PELICANS, CASPIAN TERNS, Turkey Vultures, or COMMON RAVENS. Pelagic Cormorants can be riding the waves, while Sanderlings run along the sand.

COMMON MURRE

Uria aalge

Common
Murre,
breeding
plumage

WITH THEIR STRIKING black-and-white plumage and upright posture, Common Murres are the closest things to penguins that we have in the Pacific Northwest. Their nesting colonies are among the Northwest's most amazing sensory spectacles. The smell of guano, the squawking of thousands of birds crammed in shoulder to shoulder, the mosaic of black and white that completely obscures the rock, and the aerial raids from Bald Eagles are all part of the dramatic natural display.

Murres stand upright on land, similar to their alcid relatives the puffins and the unrelated penguins. On the water, their silhouette is ducklike, but with a shorter neck and a pointier bill. During breeding season, they sport a solid black head and back with a clean, white belly. During the winter, when they are seen less frequently in the Northwest, their chins and cheeks are white, with a thin black line behind the eye.

FOOD AND FORAGING

Common Murres float on the water while resting, and they use their webbed feet to swim like a duck. When hunting under water, however, they appear to fly, diving to depths of more than 500 feet while propelling themselves with their wings. They pursue a variety of small fishes as well as squid and the occasional crustacean. An adult must eat 100 to 300 small fish per day to meet its energetic needs.

PAIRING AND PARENTING

Common Murres seem to be in no hurry to reproduce. They can live to be more than 20 years old, but they do not nest until they are 4 to 7 years of age. Females lay one egg per year and will skip a year of nesting if food availability is low or predation pressure is high. Murres nest on top of offshore rocks or on cliff ledges, often in spectacular numbers exceeding 100,000 birds. Males and females take turns incubating a single egg laid on the rocky surface. With eagles, falcons, gulls, vultures, ravens, and other predators constantly patrolling the colonies, adult murres do not leave eggs and chicks unattended unless their own safety is at risk. When the chicks are two or three weeks old, they leave the colony by jumping from their nest sites and landing in the ocean. Each chick will stay with its father at sea until it joins a flock of other murres one or two months later.

MIGRATIONS AND MOVEMENTS

Common Murres disperse from their colonies at the end of the nesting season, with colonies vacant by the end of August. During the nonbreeding season, they disperse throughout the open ocean, in bays, and in the Salish Sea. Adults visit colony areas during the winter and spring months but do not begin nesting until early May.

WHERE TO FIND COMMON MURRES

Common Murre, winter plumage

Huge aggregations of Common Murres nest on top of offshore rocks or on steep cliff ledges. You might see large numbers in the water near their colonies when they aren't nesting and smaller numbers in bays and in the Salish Sea during the winter. Look for them on top of rocks or on ledges with their thousands of neighbors during the nesting season. Some will be fishing in the water or flying over the ocean in a large flock. Even from a distance, the combination of black head, white belly, and pointed bill is distinctive.

In Washington

Cape Flattery trail near Neah Bay

Fort Worden State Park near Port Townsend

Westport and Point Brown jetties on Grays Harbor

Dungeness National Wildlife Refuge near Sequim

In Oregon

Yaquina Head Outstanding Natural Area near Newport

Heceta Head State Park near Florence

Haystack Rock in Cannon Beach

Cape Meares State Park near Oceanside

OTHER BIRDS TO SEE

Nesting Common Murres will be scanning the skies for predators. If you look up, you might see BROWN PELICANS, HEERMANN'S GULLS, PEREGRINE FALCONS, BALD EAGLES, Turkey Vultures, and COMMON RAVENS.

PIGEON GUILLEMOT

Cepphus columba

Juvenile
Pigeon
Guillemot

NO MATTER HOW dark and windy a coastal day may be, Pigeon Guillemots are out there riding the waves like intrepid surfers. They bravely dodge huge breakers and jagged rocks to find their next meal. Thanks to their big white wing patches and brightly colored feet, Pigeon Guillemots are easy to identify from a distance, even in rough weather.

In spring and summer, they are black with large white wing patches that are visible when they are floating or flying. Their brilliant red-orange feet match the lining of their mouths. In fall and winter, Pigeon Guillemots are almost entirely white on the head with some black on their wings and back. White-winged Scoters also have white wing patches but have much larger bills than guillemots, and their patches look rather small compared to those of Pigeon Guillemots when the birds are floating on the water. Common Murres and Marbled Murrelets are also black and white in winter, but these birds display more black on their heads than do Pigeon Guillemots.

Pigeon Guillemot, breeding plumage

MIGRATIONS AND MOVEMENTS

Many Pigeon Guillemots remain near the coast throughout the year, but some birds disperse after nesting, moving to the inland waters of the Salish Sea. Adults return to coastal nesting areas in March or April, and young leave the nest by the end of the summer.

WHERE TO FIND PIGEON GUILLEMOTS

Of all the alcids in the Northwest, Pigeon Guillemots are the least pelagic, or ocean-going, favoring waters close to shore. Look for them at rocky coastal areas and protected waters near fishing piers and wharves. Watch for the flash of white on their black wings as they fly low across the water.

In Washington

Cape Disappointment State Park near Ilwaco

Port Townsend area

Deception Pass State Park near Anacortes

Edmonds Pier in Edmonds

In Oregon

Yaquina Head Outstanding Natural Area near Newport

Ecola State Park near Cannon Beach

Boiler Bay State Scenic Viewpoint near Depoe Bay

Harris Beach State Park near Brookings

FOOD AND FORAGING

Pigeon Guillemots forage closer to the shore than their puffin and murre relatives and dive up to 150 feet below the surface. They use their wings and feet to propel themselves down to the rocky seafloor to probe crevices and vegetation for small fish and invertebrates such as crabs and shrimp.

PAIRING AND PARENTING

Unlike the conspicuous Common Murre, Pigeon Guillemots hide their nests in rocky crevices, earthen burrows, and structures such as wharves and bridges. Adults arrange a small mound of pebbles on which the female will lay one or two eggs. Both parents incubate during a 30-day period. Parents carry small, intact fishes for the nestlings to swallow whole. Nestlings remain in their crevice or burrow for 30 to 40 days. Once they leave the nest, young are independent and capable of swimming, diving, and catching their own food, although they cannot fly for another two or three weeks. The youngsters will not nest until they are at least three years old.

OTHER BIRDS TO SEE

Ferry docks and fishing piers are great places to get close views of birds. Look for Pelagic Cormorants, COMMON LOONS, OSPREYS, PEREGRINE FALCONS, SURF SCOTERS, and CASPIAN TERNS swimming or flying by.

MARBLED MURRELET

Brachyramphus marmoratus

Marbled Murrelet, breeding plumage

DOES ANY BIRD better embody the character of the Northwest Coast than the Marbled Murrelet? For crying out loud, it catches fish in the rough ocean waters and nests in huge, mossy trees! If it drank microbrews and wore fleece, it could be the region's mascot. This stubby little bird could use some publicity and a little help: Marbled Murrelets are currently a threatened species because of habitat loss.

This bird's common name refers to its mottled, dark brown breeding plumage. Non-breeding birds have a black cap and back with a white underside, chin, and cheek. Their stumpy body and short upright tail distinguish them from Common Murres.

FOOD AND FORAGING

Marbled Murrelets dive to depths of up to 150 feet, propelling themselves with their wings while pursuing fish or aquatic invertebrates such as shrimp. In some areas, they gather near gray whales to feast on clouds of shrimp that the whales stir up from the ocean floor.

PAIRING AND PARENTING

Marbled Murrelets are unique among our alcids because they usually lay their eggs in trees. Because they don't build a nest, they require old trees with large, mossy branches that will safely hold an egg and an incubating parent. Nest sites are 40 to 150 feet above the ground and can be more than 30 miles from oceanic feeding areas. For about 30 days, parents incubate in 24-hour shifts, with one parent relieving the other at dawn. Both parents

commute back and forth to the ocean, delivering food to the nestling until it departs the nest 27 to 40 days after hatching. After leaving the nest, young fly directly to the ocean and are independent of their parents upon arrival.

MIGRATIONS AND MOVEMENTS

Found near the Oregon and Washington coasts and in the Salish Sea throughout the year, Marbled Murrelet adults pair up in the winter and begin nesting in the spring or summer months. During the fall and winter, birds from Alaska and British Columbia mix with our year-round residents where food is plentiful in the Pacific Northwest's temperate waters.

WHERE TO FIND
MARBLES MURRELETS

Marbled Murrelets are next to impossible to find on their nesting grounds, because they come and go at dawn. Looking for them in the fall and winter is much more productive. They are easiest to find in the Salish Sea, because the water is calm and many points of land can get you close to the action. You might see them floating on the water, possibly near other alcids such as Common Murres. Marbled Murrelets

look quite small in comparison and may even disappear behind the waves.

In Washington

Fort Worden State Park near Port Townsend

Fort Flagler State Park near Port Townsend

Ediz Hook near Port Angeles

Point No Point Lighthouse and County Park near Kingston

In Oregon

Cape Meares State Park near Oceanside

Boiler Bay State Scenic Viewpoint near Depoe Bay

Siuslaw River, South Jetty, near Florence

Cook's Chasm Turnout on Cape Perpetua near Yachats

OTHER BIRDS TO SEE

Getting out on the water is a great way to see Marbled Murrelets and other alcids in the fall and winter. A boat trip off the coast of Oregon or into the Salish Sea offers amazing birding opportunities that vary with the season. You might see PIGEON GUILLEMOTS, Ancient Murrelets, TUFTED PUFFINS, Rhinoceros Auklets, Cassin's Auklets, and COMMON MURRES—and that's just the alcids.

Marbled Murrelets, winter plumage

TUFTED PUFFIN
Fratercula cirrhata

EVEN THE MOST indifferent person will wait in line behind our spotting scope to admire the comical appearance of a Tufted Puffin perched on a rock. Something about their oversized bill and hobbitlike demeanor makes them irresistible and puts them at the top of birders' Most Wanted lists. This species is the largest of America's puffins and the only one that nests on the Oregon and Washington coasts. This is a truly pelagic seabird that spends most of the year far out at sea with no land in sight, so birders eagerly await their return to their nesting sites each year.

The Tufted Puffin's large orange bill, white face, and all-black body make it very distinctive among the seabirds of the Pacific Northwest. Orange feet and yellowish feather tufts on its head complete the colorful package. Its only local relative with an orange bill is the Rhinoceros Auklet, which has a much smaller bill, lacks a white face, and is gray in color.

FOOD AND FORAGING

Fish, squid, marine worms, and shrimp are their usual fare, but they capture mostly fish when feeding their chicks. They can dive more than 200 feet below the ocean's surface in search of food, propelling themselves with their wings. They hunt alone, in small groups, or in mixed flocks with gulls, shearwaters, and murres.

PAIRING AND PARENTING

Pairs excavate burrows on soil-covered cliffs or islands. Females lay one egg in a burrow, and both parents incubate for 45 days. After the egg hatches, busy parents visit the nest to feed the nestling, sometimes with dozens of small fish draped over the sides of their bills. When the fishing is good, each parent delivers at least two billfuls to the chick each day. The amount of time the chick spends in the nest, which is dependent on the fish delivery rate, ranges from 38 to 60 days. At fledging time, the chick leaps from its burrow into the water and is no longer cared for by its parents.

MIGRATIONS AND MOVEMENTS

When summer ends, Tufted Puffins move west, spending the winter at least 60 miles off the coast in the open ocean. Each April, land-bound birders rejoice when Tufted Puffins return to their nesting colonies.

WHERE TO FIND TUFTED PUFFINS

These birds nest on islands that feature deep soil for burrowing. Look for the birds standing guard at their burrow entrances, which are usually surrounded by grass. Scan the sky around the island for frantically flapping little black footballs with white-and-orange tips—these are the Tufted Puffins.

In Washington

Protection Island, via puffin cruises at Port Townsend Marine Science Center

Offshore rocks near Neah Bay and Cape Flattery

Offshore rocks at La Push

In Oregon

Coquille Point and Face Rock near Bandon

Haystack Rock at Cannon Beach

Harris Beach State Park near Brookings

OTHER BIRDS TO SEE

An area with nesting Tufted Puffins is a great place to stay awhile and look for other birds. Sit back and watch for BALD EAGLES, HARLEQUIN DUCKS, BLACK OYSTERCATCHERS, COMMON MURRES, PIGEON GUILLEMOTS, and BROWN PELICANS.

Big Birds
EASY TO SEE AND FUN TO WATCH

BIG BIRDS CATCH your attention with their sheer size, but they will fascinate you with their dramatic exploits. While birding in the Pacific Northwest, you can watch as birds of prey (Bald and Golden Eagles) display their hunting prowess, while the world's largest songbird (Common Raven) uses its big brain to swindle a meal. Meanwhile, massive fish-eating birds (American White and Brown Pelicans) patrol the waterways in impressive flocks, and the region's tallest birds (Sandhill Cranes) leap and dance their way to nuptial bliss.

American White Pelican, winter plumage

A diverse group, these big birds have some important things in common. For example, they take longer to reach adulthood than smaller birds, and the young must wait several years before they are old enough to find a mate and nest. This might seem like a disadvantage, but these birds have a good reason to be patient: big birds live longer than small birds. In general, small birds such as hummingbirds and songbirds live less than 10 years in the wild; big birds can live for more than 20. During their long lives, big birds share parenting duties and many of them stay paired together year after year.

With the exception of the fair-weather pelicans, winter is the best time to find big numbers of big birds in the Northwest. Our winters may be damp and gray, but they are perfect for the hardy resident birds and migrants looking for ice-free water. Grab your rain gear and head out to a National Wildlife Refuge. Impress your friends and family by showing them the antics of these spectacular birds.

TRUMPETER SWAN

Cygnus buccinator

ON A CLOUD-CHOKED winter day, a small flock of huge white birds emerges from the fog. Graceful despite their large size, they seem to glow from within as they shine bright white against the dark gray northwestern sky. Their hornlike calls identify them as Trumpeter Swans. With long necks, large wings, and powerful chest muscles, they reign as the largest birds in the winter wetland. Although swans are regarded as symbols of beauty and grace, their placid behavior on the wintering grounds gives way to terrifying aggression during nesting season, delivered in the form of bites and wing blows.

In the winter, both Trumpeters and Tundra Swans visit the Pacific Northwest. The differences between the two can be subtle and are best determined with a good view. Most Tundra Swans have a patch of yellow skin between their large black bill and their eye. Trumpeters lack this yellow spot. If the two species are seen side-by-side, Trumpeters are larger, with longer necks and larger bills that seem to originate from their foreheads. The call of the Tundra Swan is more gooselike and lacks the brassiness of the Trumpeter. Similar birds include the Snow Goose, which is much smaller than either swan and has black wingtips, and the

Sandhill Crane, which is also large and light colored, but with longer legs than a swan that it extends in flight.

FOOD AND FORAGING

The Trumpeter Swan is a bird with Northwest appetites. It eats mostly vegetation but will dine on salmon carcasses and eggs, when they are abundant, each winter spawning season. Swans have a huge appetite for vegetation, eating up to 20 pounds per day. They graze on dry land like a goose or dabble for aquatic plants like a duck, tipping forward in the water and using their long necks to reach plants at the bottom of a pond.

PAIRING AND PARENTING

Male swans stay with their mates during nesting season and aggressively defend their territory, sometimes even lethally, from predators or competitors. A pair of swans works together to build a nest, a large mound at least 3 feet in diameter, with an indentation for the eggs lined with the mother's down. They build their nest on an island, a mat of floating vegetation, or a beaver lodge. The female lays four to six eggs, a small number for waterfowl, and then performs most of the incubation for 32 to 37 days, covering and warming the eggs with her feet. Young swans take a long time to grow (for a bird), about five months from being laid as an egg to flying, and will migrate with their parents during their first winter. Their parents remain together year-round.

MIGRATIONS AND MOVEMENTS

The Pacific Coast population of Trumpeter Swans nests in Alaska and migrates south for the winter in search of ice-free water. Northwestern Oregon is the southern limit of their wintering grounds. Many more spend the winter in the Salish Sea area. Trumpeters arrive in the Pacific Northwest at the end of the nesting season in October and most leave the region by March.

WHERE TO FIND TRUMPETER SWANS

Washington is the epicenter of winter Trumpeter Swan watching. They make use of the abundant fields and marshes in areas such as the Skagit Flats (in the Skagit Valley near Mount Vernon and Burlington), where they gather in large flocks. Oregon offers a few places where you can see Trumpeters in smaller numbers in the winter. Swans are so much bigger and whiter than any other waterfowl that you can literally spot them a mile away. Scan the skies and listen for their trumpet call, which sounds like a cross between a goose's honk and a child's toy horn.

In Washington

Skagit Flats, Samish Flats, and Butler Flats in Skagit County

Ridgefield National Wildlife Refuge near Vancouver

In Oregon

Fernhill Wetlands near Forest Grove

Sauvie Island near Portland

William L. Finley National Wildlife Refuge near Corvallis

OTHER BIRDS TO SEE

The combination of pastures, freshwater streams, and estuaries attracts many interesting species in large numbers to the Skagit Valley in the winter. You can see dozens of BALD EAGLES, hundreds of Snow Geese, and a higher concentration of SHORT-EARED OWLS than anywhere else in Washington. NORTHERN HARRIERS, Merlins, PRAIRIE FALCONS, and PEREGRINE FALCONS enjoy the bounty of small mammals and birds that this rich habitat provides. If you are ever going to spot an elusive Gyrfalcon, this would be a good place to do it. Also check flocks of American Wigeons for a few EURASIAN WIGEONS mixed in.

AMERICAN WHITE PELICAN

Pelecanus erythrorhynchos

WHEN IT'S SOARING, an American White Pelican seems to be all wings; its 9-foot wingspan is the largest in the Northwest. What the placid bird lacks in personality, it makes up for in fascinating group behavior. When dozens, or even hundreds, of these birds gather in flight during migration, the result is jaw-dropping. Flocks disappear and reappear as they catch the light, while spiraling upward through currents of warm air. From a distance, these huge flocks can look like a single entity; they have even been mistaken for UFOS.

The American White Pelican resembles a feathered floatplane, as it lands in the water with massive orange feet extended and then taxis around a lake. Its huge pinkish orange bill and pouch differentiate the American White from the Snow Goose, another white bird with black wingtips. The American White also has twice the wingspan of the goose and sports an upright, hornlike plate on the top of its bill during the breeding season. The similarly shaped Brown Pelican is found along the coast, unlike the inland American White.

FOOD AND FORAGING

Opportunistic foragers, American Whites mainly eat nonsport fishes such as minnows and suckers, but they will also feed on crayfish and salamanders. Look for them floating in the water and paddling around as they feed. They work in small groups to corral fish into shallow areas before scooping them up with their pouched bill, using it like a dip net. If the water is too deep, American Whites may resort to stealing fish from a deep-diving cormorant. Contrary to their cartoon image, they don't carry things in their pouch—all fish caught are immediately swallowed.

PAIRING AND PARENTING

American Whites nest east of the Cascades, abandoning and reestablishing colonies depending on water levels, predators, and food availability. They prefer to nest on islands or isolated peninsulas in freshwater or brackish lakes. Pairs pull together a shallow nest using whatever material is within bill's reach. Two eggs are incubated by both parents during a 30-day period. Eggs are insulated and protected from marauding gulls by the parents' large feet. Unlike Brown Pelican nestlings that stay in the nest for two months, American Whites leave the nest after only two or three weeks and form a group, or pod, of young. These sparsely feathered and wattled youngsters huddle together for warmth and protection while waiting for their parents to return and regurgitate a meal.

MIGRATIONS AND MOVEMENTS

These birds arrive in their eastern Oregon and Washington breeding areas in March and nest in April and May. After the nesting season, flocks disperse in all directions, and some show up on the west side of the Cascades. Some winter on the upper Columbia River, but most end up in southern California or Mexico.

American White Pelican, breeding plumage

WHERE TO FIND WHITE PELICANS

Although a few nesting sites exist in Oregon and Washington, your best chance to see American White Pelicans is to find nonbreeders or migrating birds in May to October. When present, they are easy to locate because of their huge wingspan and bright whiteness. If you don't see one, it just isn't there!

In Washington

Cassimer Bar Wildlife Area, on the Columbia River near Brewster

Gingko Petrified Forest Visitor Center, on the Columbia River near Vantage

Toppenish National Wildlife Refuge near Toppenish

Ridgefield National Wildlife Refuge near Vancouver

In Oregon

Smith and Bybee Wetlands Natural Area in Portland

Fern Ridge Wildlife Management Area near Eugene

Putnam's Point Park and Veterans Memorial Park in Klamath Falls

Crane Prairie Reservoir near La Pine

OTHER BIRDS TO SEE

You might also see fellow freshwater fish-eaters such as WESTERN GREBES, Clark's Grebes, Double-crested Cormorants, CASPIAN TERNS, Black-crowned Night-Herons, and GREAT BLUE HERONS.

BROWN PELICAN

Pelecanus occidentalis

IN THE SUMMER months, while many spring migrants to the Northwest are slaving over nests and young, Brown Pelicans are on an extended vacation. With their breeding and chick raising already finished in spring, they are free to surf the air currents above the breaking waves and preen themselves while resting on rocks. They spend a small part of the day fishing, leaving them plenty of leisure time. With their short legs and long necks, pelicans look awkward on land, but they appear confident and regal in flight with their chests puffed forward.

The American White Pelican is the only bird in this region that shares the distinctive silhouette of the Brown Pelican, but the former is extremely rare near the coast. American Whites are white with black wingtips and a bright orange bill; Brown Pelicans have a more complex coloration. Their body plumage changes color as they age, as juvenile birds exchange their brown head and white belly feathers for a white head and brown belly as adults. While on their southern nesting grounds, Brown Pelicans add a splash of bright red to their bill and pouch.

Brown
Pelican,
breeding
plumage

FOOD AND FORAGING

This large bird has a taste for small fish. Its diet along the West Coast consists primarily of anchovies, and Browns congregate where they find schools of these fish. They are the only pelicans in the world to catch their food by plunging headfirst into the water from as high as 60 feet. Their famous throat pouch expands to hold more than two-and-a-half gallons of water and fish. After they have returned to the surface, they press the pouch against their breast to drain the water out quickly before swallowing their catch. Fast and careful swallowing is important, because a Heermann's Gull might be lurking nearby, waiting to steal any fish that slip out.

PAIRING AND PARENTING

The Brown Pelicans that visit the Pacific Northwest breed on the coasts of southern California and northern Mexico. They build ground nests of kelp and sticks on rocky islands. Both parents share the incubation duties, using their large, webbed feet to regulate the temperature of two to four eggs for 30 days. Young are fed regurgitated fish for at least nine weeks until they are ready to leave the nest. They are slow to mature and do not breed until they are two or three years old.

MIGRATIONS AND MOVEMENTS

This species begins nesting in the winter and continues into spring, which is why very few Brown Pelicans are found in the Northwest during that time. Nonbreeding birds begin to appear on the Northwest Coast in May, and successful breeders arrive here in July and August. The largest groups of Browns congregate on the coast in the fall, with hundreds coming to roost together on rocks at sunset. In some years, groups of birds will stick around into the winter, although they are vulnerable to storms and food shortages.

WHERE TO FIND BROWN PELICANS

Look for Brown Pelicans near the ocean shores of Oregon and Washington. You may occasionally find them in the Salish Sea. Pelicans are large and hard to miss. They could be flying in single-file formation a foot above the waves, bobbing in the ocean, or standing on the rocks at the tip of a jetty.

In Washington

Columbia River, North Jetty, in Cape Disappointment State Park near Ilwaco

The mouth of Grays Harbor

Beaches near Ocean Park

Cape Flattery on the Olympic Peninsula

In Oregon

Columbia River, South Jetty, in Fort Stevens State Park near Astoria

Cape Kiwanda in Pacific City

Yaquina Head Outstanding Natural Area in Newport

Coquille River, South Jetty, in Bandon

OTHER BIRDS TO SEE

If you visit a jetty in August, you will be surrounded by birds and mammals taking advantage of the fish that gather where freshwater and saltwater meet. Watch for SOOTY SHEARWATERS flying past the tip of the jetty, HEERMANN'S GULLS harassing pelicans, BRANDT'S CORMORANTS and CASPIAN TERNS diving for fish, and SURF SCOTERS, COMMON MURRES, and PIGEON GUILLEMOTS floating on the waves. Look carefully for harbor seals hauled out on rocks and sea lions swimming through the water with their giant flippers.

GREAT BLUE HERON

Ardea herodias

GREAT BLUE HERONS appear graceful as they fly with deep wing beats or tiptoe through shallow water. When hunting, however, they are the Terminator on stilts. A Great Blue's stone-faced expression betrays no emotion as a fish, snake, or rodent wriggles in its sharp bill before being swallowed alive. Watching a heron on a hunt is a great chance to see Tennyson's "nature, red in tooth and claw" (and beak) in action.

Although they superficially resemble cranes, Great Blues' beaks are longer and sharper, they tuck in their necks during flight, and they are more likely to be solitary. When in flight, herons bear a resemblance to the long-extinct pterodactyl.

FOOD AND FORAGING

The classic image of a Great Blue Heron is wading in the water, eyes focused downward, looking for fish. Its long, pointed beak is well suited for this type of feeding, but it actually eats a wide variety of prey. A short list of heron meals would include snakes, frogs, crayfish, rodents, and small birds. A heron hunts by stalking so slowly that you might find it difficult to see its movement. It strikes quickly by uncoiling its long neck and shooting its bill toward the water or the ground. After capturing an animal in its bill, a heron repositions the creature with a series of tosses so that it can be swallowed headfirst.

PAIRING AND PARENTING

Although they prefer to feed alone, Great Blues will build a stick nest just a few feet away from another heron in arboreal rookeries. They begin the breeding process with an elaborate display in their nest trees, which involves the male transferring sticks to the female as she creates the nest, and both sexes making clacking noises with their bills. Stick nests can be reused each year and can grow quite large; a group of birds will sometimes abandon rookeries, however, and start new ones. Great Blues lay two to six eggs and incubate them for 27 days. In spring and summer, you can hear nestlings from the ground when they squawk loudly as their parents return to the nest with food.

MIGRATIONS AND MOVEMENTS

Great Blue Herons remain in the Pacific Northwest year-round in areas where the water doesn't freeze during winter months. Their long nesting season begins when adults begin occupying rookeries in February or March and ends when young herons leave their nests in June or July.

WHERE TO FIND GREAT BLUE HERONS

Given the Great Blue's varied diet, it is not surprising that they can thrive in many different kinds of habitats. They are often found near water, whether a pond in a park or a mudflat in a coastal bay. They hunt land-dwelling prey as well, so keep an eye out for them hunting in fields when you are driving through farm country. If you are looking for Great Blues in a lake or pond and don't see one initially, scan the edge of the water with binoculars; you might spot one hunched up and motionless, looking like a stick. Unlike cranes, all herons, as well as their relatives, the egrets, are capable of perching in trees and will do so frequently throughout the year. Great Blues are common and widely distributed in Oregon and Washington, but rookeries can be difficult to find.

In Washington

Dumas Bay Sanctuary in Federal Way

University of Washington campus, Rainier Vista

Lake Sammamish State Park near Issaquah

In Oregon

Ross Island in the Willamette River, viewed from the South Waterfront area of Portland

Goat Island in the Willamette River, viewed from Maddax Woods in West Linn

Sturgeon Lake on Sauvie Island near Portland

OTHER BIRDS TO SEE

A springtime visit to a rookery could also produce BALD EAGLES, OSPREYS, Double-crested Cormorants, Pied-billed Grebes, and Common Mergansers. An abandoned nest could hold a family of GREAT HORNED OWLS.

BALD EAGLE

Haliaeetus leucocephalus

Adult Bald Eagle

PERCHING WITH PERFECTLY upright posture in a dead tree, a pair of Bald Eagles looks out over the marsh that makes up their kingdom. Their huge yellow beaks and feet the size of human hands make their predatory abilities obvious. They communicate with piercing calls that do not resemble those of a Red-tailed Hawk, but are more similar to a gull's screams. Suddenly the larger female dives down over the marsh, and a panicked cloud of ducks and geese scatters into the sky.

An adult Bald Eagle is unmistakable. Both perched and in flight, the pattern of white head, dark brown body and wings, and white tail is recognizable even at great distances. Immature Bald Eagles in brownish plumage can be confused with other large dark birds such as Golden Eagles, Red-tailed Hawks, and Turkey Vultures. Don't forget that juvenile eagles, and most other birds, are at least as large as their parents by the time they leave the nest.

FOOD AND FORAGING

Large, sharp talons and hooked beaks are ideally suited to catching and eating meat. Bald Eagles are known for plucking fish out of the water, but their diet is diverse. They frequently hunt mammals, ducks, gulls, and seabirds. They also scavenge dead mammals, fish, and even the placentas of seals and farm animals. With a confident posture and an intense gaze, the Bald Eagle appears dignified even as it eats something most of us would bury.

PAIRING AND PARENTING

Bald Eagles often reuse the same nest year after year, adding more sticks each season. They make the largest nests of any North American bird, which can measure 9 feet across and weigh more than 2 tons. They often build their nests in tall deciduous trees such as black cottonwoods. Females lay one to three eggs and both parents incubate for 34 to 36 days, but the number of young that leave the nest depends on the amount of food available. Young leave the nest in brown plumage and must wait at least four years to develop the famous white head and tail.

Juvenile Bald Eagle

MIGRATIONS AND MOVEMENTS

The Pacific Northwest is a popular winter destination for Bald Eagles that arrive from the north after salmon have stopped spawning in Alaska and British Columbia. Areas with large concentrations of fish and ducks attract the largest numbers of migrants, which begin arriving in November. Wintering Bald Eagles compete for food and share their evening roosts with the resident eagles that stay year-round. Eagles nesting in the Northwest begin constructing or renovating their nests in late winter and fledge their young by late summer.

WHERE TO FIND BALD EAGLES

Bald Eagles nest in the Pacific Northwest, but you can find them any time of year; in winter they gather in large groups in places where prey is abundant. They are often quite conspicuous, especially the adults, with their contrasting dark brown and white plumage. Scan prominent perches such as snags and large branches near water for a large, upright bird.

In Washington

The Upper Skagit River near Rockport

San Juan Islands and along the nearby ferry routes, perched in trees and in the air

Ridgefield National Wildlife Refuge near Vancouver

In Oregon

Sauvie Island near Portland

Klamath Basin around Klamath Falls

Netarts Bay near Netarts

Ankeny National Wildlife Refuge near Albany

OTHER BIRDS TO SEE

Oregon's Klamath Basin in the winter is a hotspot for birds. In addition to huge roosts of eagles, you might see PRAIRIE FALCONS, Rough-legged Hawks, RUDDY DUCKS, Greater White-fronted Geese, Horned Larks, and COMMON RAVENS.

GOLDEN EAGLE

Aquila chrysaetos

IT ISN'T THAT a Golden Eagle would eat a small child; it's just that it could if it wanted to. How could you not be impressed by a bird large and ambitious enough to hunt mammals such as antelope and deer? Their formidable talons dwarf even those of the Bald Eagle, and they are one of the top predators of the dry open country.

The massive size of Golden Eagles differentiates them from most other birds of prey. Their habitat is usually different from that of brown juvenile Bald Eagles that prefer water, but in areas where the two do overlap, you can look for the relatively smaller head and golden nape on Goldens.

FOOD AND FORAGING

The Golden is a skilled hunter with amazing distance vision. It occasionally captures birds, but mammals such as rabbits, hares, and rodents make up the bulk of its diet. Goldens also kill alarmingly large prey such as pronghorn antelope, bighorn sheep, and Sandhill Cranes. They use their talons to grasp an animal after pouncing from above, sometimes while hunting in pairs.

PAIRING AND PARENTING

Golden Eagles are more likely than Bald Eagles to construct nests on cliffs, although they will nest in trees if necessary. The female does most of the incubation of one to three eggs for 43 to 45 days. Both parents care for nestlings. The amount of time young spend in the nest varies from 45 to 80 days and depends on their growth rate, which is influenced the amount of rodents, rabbits, and jackrabbits their parents are able to catch. By the time the eaglets fledge, their nest is an unsanitary pile of mammalian remains and the insects they've attracted. Perhaps to allow things to freshen up, pairs often maintain multiple nest sites, alternating use between years.

MIGRATIONS AND MOVEMENTS

Northern populations of Goldens are migratory, and many of these birds are spotted in western Oregon and Washington as they travel from Alaskan and Canadian nesting grounds to their southern wintering areas. In the eastern parts of Oregon and Washington, you can see them year-round. Our resident Goldens begin nesting in late winter or early spring and stay at their nests until the youngsters fledge in the summer.

WHERE TO FIND GOLDEN EAGLES

Birds of the open country, Goldens are more common on the east side of the Cascades. They are always a treat to find, because they are never a sure thing. They hunt from the air but also from perches such as utility poles. They are easily distinguished from other raptors by their massive size. If you aren't sure, your mystery raptor is probably a hawk, not an eagle.

In Washington

Yakima Canyon and surrounding areas
     near Yakima

Hurricane Ridge in Olympic National Park
     (summer and early fall)

In Oregon

Smith Rock State Park near Redmond (nesting)

Fort Rock State Park near La Pine

OTHER BIRDS TO SEE

Go to Smith Rock State Park in May or June to check out nesting Golden Eagles, and stick around to enjoy the PRAIRIE FALCONS, White-throated Swifts, CALIFORNIA QUAIL, WESTERN KINGBIRDS, Say's Phoebes, CANYON WRENS, and Black-billed Magpies.

SANDHILL CRANE

Grus canadensis

THE TRUE BEGINNING of fall is the first crisp morning when you hear the haunting call of a flock of Sandhill Cranes making their way south. Their unmistakable call, something like a cross between a raven and a goose, carries far on chilly mornings. When they spot a mown cornfield, they resemble skydivers, landing effortlessly on cupped wings. Despite their reputation as graceful dancers, they will charge, peck, and hiss to protect their offspring.

Sandhill Cranes are the tallest birds in the Northwest, with some individuals reaching more than 4 feet in height. Adults are light pearly gray with a small red cap, and juveniles,

or colts, are a rusty brown color. Cranes fly with both their necks and legs extended, distinguishing them from herons and egrets that fly with tucked necks. Herons are also different in that they have sharp, stabbing beaks and hunt by stalking. Cranes feed in a grazing manner with blunt beaks. Geese also have long necks, but their shorter legs are not as visible in flight as a Sandhill Crane's outstretched legs.

FOOD AND FORAGING

Sandhill Cranes are true omnivores and use their long, flexible bills to eat nearly anything, plant or animal, they find on the ground or in shallow water. They thrive in many areas because of their appetite for corn and other crops. Corn provides sugar and fat to fuel migration, but females must consume protein in the form of earthworms and other invertebrates to prepare for laying eggs. They also feed on insects, voles, and bird eggs at their northern nesting grounds where plants are scarce.

PAIRING AND PARENTING

Elaborate dances help attract a mate or reinforce the Sandhill's bond with its partner, with whom it pairs until death. These displays involve a lot of calling, hopping, head-tossing, and plant-flinging. The dances begin on the wintering grounds and escalate during migration as adults prepare to return to the nesting grounds.

Sandhills need wet meadows for nesting. They build a floating nest on a mat of vegetation to discourage predation by raccoons and skunks. Pairs nest during the late spring and early summer. Both parents incubate two eggs for 30 days and take care of the often solitary fledgling, or colt, that survives. The family travels together until the next nesting season, when the colt will join a group of youngsters. The colt will stay in this group until it is old enough to mate, for up to six years.

MIGRATIONS AND MOVEMENTS

If you know where to look, you'll find Sandhill Cranes throughout the year in the Pacific Northwest. Those that nest in Oregon and Washington spend the spring and summer in the region and spend the winter in California's Central Valley. Those that we see migrating through western Oregon and Washington in the fall have likely bred in Canada and Alaska. Some of them stay in the Portland and Vancouver, Washington, area all winter, but the majority head farther south.

WHERE TO FIND SANDHILL CRANES

In a few places in Oregon and Washington, you can catch an exciting glimpse of a small, rusty brown colt following its parents around a meadow. Just as impressive are the large, vocal flocks of Sandhill Cranes that spend the winter near the Columbia River. You'll probably hear them before you see them. During migration, Sandhills fly in an orderly wedge, but when they are looking for a landing place, they will soar without flapping and circle the area. If you are lucky, you'll get to watch them parachute to the ground on outstretched wings, landing so daintily that they seem to step out of the sky. On the ground, check meadows and farm fields, especially those with corn stalk stubble.

In Washington

Ridgefield National Wildlife Refuge near Vancouver (winter)

Conboy Lake National Wildlife Refuge near Glenwood (nesting)

In Oregon

Sauvie Island near Portland (winter)

Klamath Marsh National Wildlife Refuge near Klamath Falls (nesting)

Davis Lake near La Pine (nesting)

OTHER BIRDS TO SEE

Winter is a great time to bird the wildlife refuges and wetlands of the Portland and Vancouver areas. A visit to Sauvie Island or Ridgefield National Wildlife Refuge can produce CACKLING GEESE, Snow Geese, TRUMPETER SWANS, BALD EAGLES, PEREGRINE FALCONS, and GREAT BLUE HERONS near the water. RED-TAILED HAWKS, NORTHERN HARRIERS, Rough-legged Hawks, and American Kestrels search the fields for voles.

COMMON RAVEN

Corvus corax

THERE MUST BE some special affinity between Common Ravens and humans. How else can you explain the long history of these birds in art and stories, or the stirring that you feel in your chest when a raven's call echoes across a wild place? Ravens have a certain dignity and confidence in their demeanor and intelligence in their eyes that draws you in and makes you want to stay and watch them a little longer.

Crows are the birds most likely to be confused with Common Ravens, because both are solid glossy black. Luckily, you can tell them apart by differences in their appearances and their calls. A crow says "caw," but a Common Raven has a hoarser voice and says "quorrk." Crows are smaller and have fan-shaped tails. Ravens are larger, actually the largest songbird in the world, and have diamond-shaped tails. They often soar with their wings and tail fanned out, while crows always flap when flying. The Turkey Vulture is another dark bird that soars, but its head is featherless, it has silvery feathers under its wings, and it soars with its wings in a V shape (V is for vulture).

FOOD AND FORAGING

Ravens use their wits to acquire a wide variety of foods, mostly meat, through scavenging, hunting, and stealing. These wily birds often work together to steal bird eggs or catch prey. Ever the problem solvers, ravens will follow large predators to a meal and will even try to attract them to a dying animal that they can't open up on their own. Their bills are strong enough to crack a walnut but are not sharp enough to rip into a squirrel.

PAIRING AND PARENTING

Ravens collect sticks to construct their large nests and line them with scavenged fur, grass, paper, and bark. They are very flexible about where they nest: a cliff, a barn, a tree, or a power pole will do, as long as there is sufficient food nearby for the hungry nestlings that need a constant supply of insects and meat to thrive. They lay three to seven eggs and incubate for at least 20 days. Baby ravens, naked and big-mouthed, will never win a cuteness contest. The age at which young leave the nest depends on the rate of food delivered by their parents and ranges from four to seven weeks. After leaving the nest, the youngsters wander for several years and may join nomadic flocks before finding a mate and settling down to nest.

MIGRATIONS AND MOVEMENTS

Ravens don't have a regular seasonal migration, but some wander after the breeding season to find food bonanzas and roosting sites. Breeding pairs nest in the spring and summer and remain together throughout the rest of the year.

WHERE TO FIND COMMON RAVENS

Common Ravens can be found throughout Oregon and Washington, but populations are concentrated in the Cascades. A great way to spot a raven flying overhead, perched in a tree, or walking along a road is to drive up a mountain pass and stop for a picnic or a hike. A long walk along the beach may produce a raven sighting as well. Some of the most difficult places to find a raven are the big cities along the Interstate 5 corridor: Portland, Tacoma, and Seattle. When you're traveling through mountains, deserts, or coastal areas, listen for the "quorrk" of distant ravens. Scan the sky for the diamond-shaped tail of a flying raven and check the ground in open areas and along roadsides. Remember that these birds love roadkill.

OTHER BIRDS TO SEE

If you pull off a mountain highway to get a good look at a Common Raven, roll your window down and look for other birds as well, such as Steller's Jays, Dark-eyed Juncos, and VARIED THRUSHES that take advantage of open areas in the forest. Listen for forest birds such as PACIFIC WRENS, RED-BREASTED NUT-HATCHES, and RED-BREASTED SAPSUCKERS.

Colorful Birds
BRIGHTENING THE PACIFIC NORTHWEST

MANY BIRDS THAT STAY year-round in the Northwest keep with a neutral dress code, but each spring we get an influx of vivid color in the form of migrants that light up our wetlands and forests. These dazzling travelers join a few bright resident birds to create an avian rainbow. In one wonderful day, you could see the rosy red of a noisy flock of crossbills, the copper-penny orange of a male Rufous Hummingbird, the aptly-named Yellow-headed Blackbird, and the rich hues of a swooping Violet-green Swallow. Although each of these birds has more going for it than just its color, the vibrant colors are what will stick in your memory and cheer you during the dark days of winter.

Male Lazuli Bunting

WOOD DUCK

Aix sponsa

IT SEEMS THAT an overzealous artist designed the Wood Duck by adding another flourish one time too many. You might think that you'd have to travel the globe to find a duck with this amazing combination of colors and patterns. In fact, the most ornate of the pond-dwellers is a native bird, not an exotic escapee. The Wood Duck drake is pretty humble considering his good looks. He is more likely to be found perching quietly on a log along the edge of a pond than flaunting his handsomeness out in the open.

The male is unmistakable, with his iridescent feathered head, eye outlined in red, yellow and red bill, and speckled chestnut-colored breast. Females are attractive in their own way, with a teardrop-shaped white patch surrounding each eye. Wood Duck head feathers form a helmet shape and their wings show a bit of iridescence.

FOOD AND FORAGING

These omnivorous birds feed in the water or on dry land. Common foods include aquatic vegetation, swimming insects, grass seeds, acorns, and fruits. Orchards, vineyards, and farms that border wooded, watery habitats are attractive feeding sites for Wood Ducks.

PAIRING AND PARENTING

Males accompany females much of the year, but they provide no parental care of young, leaving the female when she begins incubating. The female selects a nest site high above the ground, usually a tree cavity or a nest box. She lines the cavity with her down and lays ten or more eggs, incubating them for 30 days. Females often lay eggs in the nests of other Wood Ducks, perhaps to hedge their bets against nest failure. Less than two days after hatching, ducklings must leap several stories from their nest to join their calling mother on the ground and search for food. Luckily, they flutter and bounce to land safely.

MIGRATIONS AND MOVEMENTS

Wood Ducks are early breeders, with pairing beginning in late summer and nesting beginning in late winter in many areas. Northern populations are migratory, and many pass through Washington and Oregon on their way to California. Large gatherings congregate in Oregon and Washington in the fall when southbound migrants mix with year-round residents in wooded streams and ponds.

WHERE TO FIND WOOD DUCKS

Wood Ducks are widespread across the western portions of Oregon and Washington in ponds and lakes. For such an ostentatious bird, they can be surprisingly difficult to see. Look in the shadows along the edges of ponds and on logs near the water.

In Washington

Yakima Sportsman State Park in Yakima

Nisqually National Wildlife Refuge near Olympia

Male (left) and female Wood Ducks

Juanita Bay Park in Kirkland

Kent Ponds in the Green River Natural Resources Area near Seattle

In Oregon

Crystal Springs Rhododendron Garden in Portland

Smith and Bybee Wetlands Natural Area in Portland

Dawson Creek Corporate Park in Hillsboro

Ashland Pond in Ashland

Delta Ponds along the Willamette River in Eugene

Minto-Brown Island Park in Salem

OTHER BIRDS TO SEE

A willow-lined pond may yield more birds than what first appears. GREEN HERONS perch just above the water; Pied-billed Grebes, Green-winged Teals, and HOODED MERGANSERS swim quietly, while a WILSON'S WARBLER skulks in the shrubs, revealed only by its call.

CINNAMON TEAL

Anas cyanoptera

WHEN YOU'RE BIRDING a wetland in late spring, scan the vegetated edges of ponds for the shy but stunning Cinnamon Teal, which avoids open water. Your persistence will pay off when you get to see the juxtaposition of red duck, green grass, and blue sky. These graceful swimmers and swift flyers are the highlight of many a wetland birding trip. Cinnamon Teals are truly western ducks that favor the marshes of intermountain valleys. They have been living in this area since the last Ice Age.

Males are unmistakable swimming or in flight, with their brick-red bodies and turquoise wing patches. If you get a great look, you'll see that even the male's eyes are red. Females are not cinnamon-colored, so they look very similar to Blue-winged Teals, with their brown plumage and blue wing patches. Ruddy Ducks are a similar shade of red but have white cheeks and blue bills.

FOOD AND FORAGING

Cinnamon Teals are in the group of ducks known as dabblers, of which Mallards are the most familiar. Dabblers rarely dive completely under water. Instead, they tip head-down and bottom-up to reach submerged plants and animals. Dabblers also pick food from the water's surface or peck at food on dry land.

PAIRING AND PARENTING

Hens construct nests in wetland vegetation, often placing them just above the water on islands or tufts of plants. Some nests are hidden under a mat of dead vegetation that functions as a roof to shield the eggs from predators. The hen incubates a large clutch of up to 16 eggs for at least 21 days. Ducklings are difficult to find, because hens are experts at hiding them from you or any other animal they perceive as a predator.

MIGRATIONS AND MOVEMENTS

This species nests throughout the Pacific Northwest, but most Cinnamons spend the winter in California or Latin American. Pairs arrive at Northwest nesting grounds in the late winter or early spring and depart the region in late summer or early fall. Males are the first to fly south, leaving the nesting grounds while the hens are incubating their eggs.

WHERE TO FIND CINNAMON TEALS

Look for Cinnamon Teals in low-elevation ponds and wetland complexes. As sneaky as the bird tries to be, its bright rusty color gives it away. Scan the edge of the water to see this beautiful duck hiding among the grass tufts and cattails.

In Washington

Ridgefield National Wildlife Refuge near Vancouver (year-round)

Toppenish National Wildlife Refuge near Yakima

Nisqually National Wildlife Refuge near Olympia

Male (left) and female Cinnamon Teals

Spencer Island Park, part of the Snohomish River Estuary, near Everett

In Oregon

Killin Wetlands near Banks

Klamath Marsh National Wildlife Refuge near Klamath Falls

Fern Ridge Wildlife Management Area near Eugene

William L. Finley National Wildlife Refuge near Corvallis

OTHER BIRDS TO SEE

The tall plants in a summer marsh hide many secretive birds. You'll need keen eyes and ears to find Soras, Marsh Wrens, AMERICAN BITTERNS, Wilson's Snipes, and Common Yellowthroats.

RUDDY DUCK

Oxyura jamaicensis

Male Ruddy Duck, breeding plumage

FOOD AND FORAGING

Ruddies are insect-eating specialists, more so than other ducks. They dive to the bottom of ponds and probe their spatulalike bill into the sediment to filter out aquatic insects and other invertebrates. Plant matter becomes a larger part of their diet during the winter when insects are scarce.

PAIRING AND PARENTING

Unlike most ducks that arrive already paired, Ruddies wait until they arrive on nesting grounds to find a mate. Upon arrival, the male performs a comical bubble display to attract a female. He rapidly beats his bill downward against his chest to make bubbles in the water, creating clicking and gurgling sounds. Next, he lengthens his body while making a "boing" sound and then repeats the process. Ruddy Duck eggs are odd in that they are proportionately larger than those of other ducks and have a surprisingly rough exterior. Females incubate five to ten eggs for 23 days. Ducklings are highly developed and can dive for and catch insects a day after hatching.

SMALL BUT PUGNACIOUS and extroverted, the Ruddy Duck chases away just about anything from its breeding territory, performing unforgettable displays to intimidate rivals and woo a mate. His tough guy act is even funnier coming from a duck with the body type of a squeaky bath toy. Small and round with a stubby bill and tail, he must think he looks more like a swan.

During breeding season, males are a warm, cinnamon color with a bill as blue as the summer sky. A black cap, white cheek, and tipped-up tail complete the picture of this cocky little duck. During the winter, when other ducks are sporting their brightest plumage, male Ruddies fade to a dull brown but are identifiable by their light cheeks and often erect tail. Females have the same compact shape, but they are brown all year with an indistinct stripe across each cheek.

MIGRATIONS AND MOVEMENTS

Ruddy Ducks reside in Oregon and Washington throughout the year. During the May to August nesting season, they are most abundant in marshes east of the Cascade Crest. They switch sides during the nonbreeding season, with greater numbers west of the Cascades.

Male Ruddy Duck, winter plumage

WHERE TO FIND RUDDY DUCKS

The Northwest offers a variety of places to find Ruddy Ducks. During the winter, scan bays and lakes for mixed flocks of diving ducks, such as Buffleheads and scaup, that Ruddies often join. In the breeding season, look for displaying males in patches of open water surrounded by vegetation. Their cinnamon color contrasts well with the green backdrop.

In Washington

Crockett Lake on Whidbey Island (winter)

Lake Terrel near Bellingham (winter)

Ridgefield National Wildlife Refuge near Vancouver (year-round)

Toppenish National Wildlife Refuge near Yakima (summer)

In Oregon

Yaquina Bay in Newport (winter)

Jackson Bottom Wetlands Preserve near Hillsboro (winter)

Ankeny National Wildlife Refuge near Albany (winter)

Klamath Falls area (year-round)

OTHER BIRDS TO SEE

Marshes east of the Cascades are full of exciting birds during the breeding season. You might see YELLOW-HEADED BLACKBIRDS and Virginia Rails among the cattails, and Black Terns and COMMON NIGHTHAWKS swooping overhead.

BAND-TAILED PIGEON

Patagioenas fasciata

IF IT'S POSSIBLE to look both regal and awkward at the same time, the Band-tailed Pigeon does it. Its puffed chest and intricate markings contrast with its ungainly, fast-flapping takeoffs and precarious treetop landings to humorous effect. These large, purple invaders of bird feeders are a delight to watch as they crowd for a bite of birdseed or flap loudly through the forest.

This species looks like a city pigeon that has been customized. To visualize a Band-tailed Pigeon, start with a familiar Rock Pigeon (city pigeon), and add a yellow bill, yellow feet, and a thick, light gray band at the end of the tail. Finish the masterpiece with a white band and an iridescent patch at the nape of the neck.

FOOD AND FORAGING

Humans aren't the only Northwest residents practicing seasonal eating. Band-tailed Pigeons are strict plant-eaters that will fly many miles to obtain whatever fruits, flowers, and seeds are available in forests. Breeding adults will travel up to 30 miles from their nest sites to find a good crop of an abundant food, such as red elderberry. Birds in a flock hang acrobatically from branches to pluck berries, acorns, or other plant parts, working their way from the top to the bottom of a tree. Flocks regularly gather at salt-rich springs, saltwater estuaries, and exposed mineral deposits to consume sodium and other nutrients needed to balance their berry-rich diet.

PAIRING AND PARENTING

The Band-tailed arranges a handful of twigs into a simple stack at least 5 feet off the ground in a tree and calls it a nest. Females lay only one egg per nest attempt, but pairs can successfully nest three times per year. Both parents incubate the egg for about 20 days and produce crop milk, a product unique to doves and pigeons that is secreted into an enlarged chamber of the adult esophagus and then regurgitated for their nestling. Crop milk is eventually replaced by adult food before the chick leaves the nest, 25 to 29 days after hatching.

MIGRATIONS AND MOVEMENTS

Migratory flocks are formed in September and travel from the Northwest to California. Their flight schedules are dictated by the presence of fruits and flowers encountered along the way. They return to our region by March to begin nesting. Some individuals have become permanent residents of urban areas thanks to a year-round supply of food at bird feeders.

WHERE TO FIND BAND-TAILED PIGEONS

These denizens of moist forests are found throughout western Oregon and Washington but are much less common east of the Cascades. At first light, you can find Band-tailed Pigeons perching on the skinny tops of coniferous trees. During the day, look for their bulky shapes flapping over the treetops or at a feeder in a tree-filled neighborhood.

In Washington

Olympic National Park

Willapa National Wildlife Refuge near South
  Bend

Julia Butler Hansen Refuge near Cathlamet

Lake Sammamish State Park near Issaquah

In Oregon

Pittock Mansion in Portland

Mount Tabor Park in Portland

Scoggins Valley Park near Forest Grove

William L. Finley National Wildlife Refuge
  near Corvallis

Fort Stevens State Park near Astoria

Larch Mountain near Troutdale

OTHER BIRDS TO SEE

A forest hike in late spring can produce a long list of wonderful birds such as PILEATED WOODPECKERS, OLIVE-SIDED FLYCATCHERS, RED CROSSBILLS, SWAINSON'S THRUSHES, and even Northern Pygmy Owls.

RUFOUS HUMMINGBIRD

Selasphorus rufus

Male
Rufous
Hummingbird

Male hummingbirds in the Northwest are pretty simple to tell apart. The Rufous, whose name means reddish, is orange with a copper-colored throat; the Anna's is green with a fuchsia helmet; and the Calliope is green with a purple-streaked throat. Females are trickier to tell apart, but the Rufous has a green back, orangeish flanks, and a clean white stripe separating the neck and belly. If you want to earn a Ph.D. in hummingbird identification, go to the southern Oregon Coast and tease apart the Rufous and Allen's Hummingbirds, whose ranges overlap in this area.

FOOD AND FORAGING

Using their bills and tongues to reach nectar in flowers, Rufouses also drink sap from wells carved in trees by sapsuckers. They capture small insects in the air and glean insects from vegetation. Their tiny brains show a great capacity for spatial memory, as demonstrated by banded individuals returning to the exact locations of feeding sites year after year.

PAIRING AND PARENTING

Males arrive at nesting grounds before females and begin to perform aerial displays. The male flies dozens of feet above the ground; then descends rapidly, pulling up at the last second to make a J-shape; and then flies to a new point in the sky to repeat the process. When a female is attracted, the male will shuffle back-and-forth near the branch on which she is perched. The female then begins building her nest immediately upon arrival at the nesting grounds. The nest is a tiny, cozy work of art: a small cup lined with downy material and an exterior decorated with green moss and

WE KNOW THAT spring has arrived (or is at least on its way) when we first hear the zing of a flying Rufous Hummingbird. Each year they return from the south to chase away the resident Anna's Hummingbirds from the feeders they've frequented all winter. Though smaller than the Anna's, the Rufous is a feisty hummingbird not afraid to act as if it owns every feeder. They arrive just in time to take advantage of the particular plants, such as red huckleberry and red currant, that begin to flower quite early in our mild climate.

mint-colored lichens, all held together with spider webs. The female alone incubates her two coffee-bean–sized eggs for about 16 days and then regurgitates meals for the nestlings during the 21 days they are in the nest. Like other hummingbird young, Rufous nestlings are competent flyers as soon as they fledge.

MIGRATIONS AND MOVEMENTS

If you measure migration distance in body length instead of miles or kilometers, the Rufous Hummingbird migrates the longest distance in the bird world. Most spend their winters in southern California or Mexico and then perform an elliptical migration: flying north along the coast in spring to reach north-western nesting sites, and then flying south along the Rocky Mountains in the fall, back to their winter grounds. Rufouses travel this route to feed on flowers that peak in spring along the West Coast and in late summer in the Rockies. Of the many that show up in the Northwest in February or March, some will stick around to nest, but most will continue north to British Columbia or Alaska.

Female
Rufous
Hummingbird

WHERE TO FIND RUFOUS HUMMINGBIRDS

Late March and early April are the best times to find large numbers of Rufouses at the peak of migration. Fill up your feeder and get ready for a show. Later on, during nesting season, they prefer places with a mix of large trees, shrubs, and open areas. Unless you are watching a bird feeder, you'll often locate a Rufous by its sound. With a little practice, you will easily recognize the metallic flight sounds of males zooming by. Anna's vocalize but don't make the same sounds in flight, which simplifies things. Also check thin branches at the tops of trees for territorial males.

In Washington

Blackbird Island in Leavenworth

Skagit Wildlife Area near Mount Vernon

Marymoor Park in Redmond

Kent Ponds in the Green River Natural
    Resources Area near Seattle

Bottle Beach State Park near Westport

In Oregon

Pittock Mansion in Portland

Audubon Society of Portland's Nature
    Sanctuary near Forest Park

Scoggins Valley Park near Forest Grove

Clay Myers State Natural Area near Pacific City

Beaver Creek State Natural Area near Newport

Ankeny National Wildlife Refuge near Albany

William L. Finley National Wildlife Refuge
    near Corvallis

OTHER BIRDS TO SEE

A marsh surrounded by tall trees is attractive to Rufous Hummingbirds and also provides a wonderful variety of habitats for BLACK-HEADED GROSBEAKS, WESTERN TANAGERS, Black-throated Gray Warblers, Purple Finches, and CEDAR WAXWINGS.

CALLIOPE HUMMINGBIRD

Selasphorus calliope

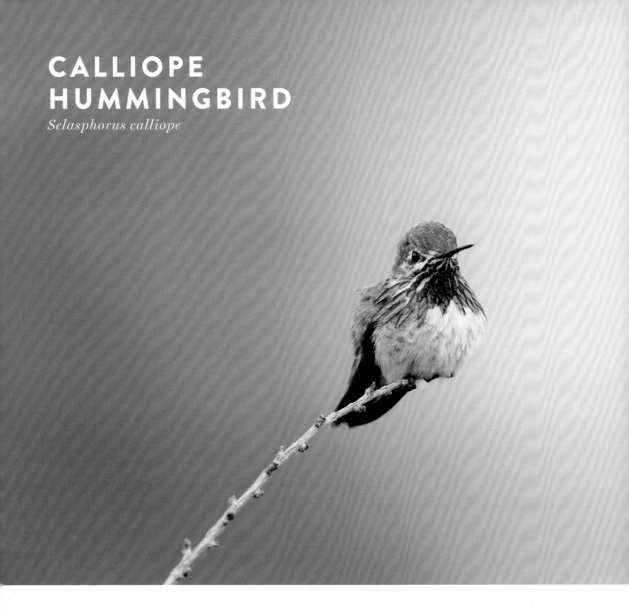

Male
Calliope
Hummingbird

YOU WOULD THINK that the smallest breeding bird in North America would want to hide, but male Calliope Hummingbirds make themselves known by diving through the air, buzzing loudly, and flaring iridescent feathers to the side for all to see. All of this excitement comes in a tiny package; these birds weigh no more than a stick of gum.

The male Calliope has a gorget, a patch of iridescent feathers on its throat and head, unlike any other hummer found in this region. Instead of a solid iridescent patch, it has purplish iridescent stripes on its white throat. The female closely resembles a female Rufous Hummingbird: greenish and rufous (reddish) with a white belly.

FOOD AND FORAGING

The Calliope has a diet similar to that of other hummingbirds: nectar, insects, and sap. As a forest gap specialist, this species regularly feeds on flowering plants in sunny mountain meadows and streamside areas.

PAIRING AND PARENTING

Males establish breeding territories in open areas with prominent perches, usually the tips of willow stems that have died back. Males perform U-shaped aerial displays by hovering dozens of feet above the ground, diving, climbing, and hovering at another location, repeated as necessary to attract females. The male produces sounds with his feathers during the dive and creates a high-pitched buzz from his bill while hovering in front of a female attracted by his display. If she approves, they will fly together and spin in an aerial circle, joining together with their bills. The female usually constructs her nest on the branch of a pine tree, with the nest arranged to resemble a pinecone. The female incubates her two eggs for about 15 days and feeds the young a diet composed mainly of insects for the 18 to 21 days that they are in the nest.

MIGRATIONS AND MOVEMENTS

Calliopes have a migration pattern similar to Rufous Hummingbirds, with northbound spring migration occurring over low elevations and coastal areas, and southbound fall migration occurring over higher elevations. The spring arrival of Calliopes in the Northwest is subtler than that of the Rufous because of the Calliope's less aggressive nature, smaller size, and superficial similarity to the ubiquitous Anna's Hummingbird. Calliopes typically arrive in the Northwest in April or May and have departed for their winter grounds by September. Males, which provide no parental care, leave nesting areas before females and young and often disperse throughout the Northwest prior to heading south.

WHERE TO FIND CALLIOPE HUMMINGBIRDS

Calliope Hummingbirds are easiest to find on their nesting grounds in late May or early June, when males are displaying. Check the spindly dead twigs at the tops of willows or other shrubs along streams in high-elevation meadows. Watch for something the size of a big bee flying around, and you might get to see the Calliope's U-shaped display flight as well.

In Washington

Along the Goldendale-Bickleton Highway northeast of The Dalles, Oregon

Wenas Campground (Audubon Campground) near Ellensburg

Upper Skagit River near Newhalem

In Oregon

Calliope Crossing near Sisters

Crater Lake National Park

OTHER BIRDS TO SEE

A visit to Calliope country can also produce Red-naped Sapsuckers, Northern Goshawks, Pinyon Jays, and GREEN-TAILED TOWHEES.

WESTERN KINGBIRD
Tyrannus verticalis

THE WESTERN KINGBIRD is the most conspicuous of the flycatchers in the Northwest, with its lemon-yellow belly and habit of perching on transmission wires in open areas. This aggressive bird will chase just about anything and has no desire to hide from attention. Its whole life is an open book, from the insect-catching show held in open fields to the nesting performance conducted atop a utility pole.

A bright yellow belly and gray head distinguish this flycatcher from similar birds, such as the Western Meadowlark, with its white-edged tail and yellow breast; the meadowlark also has a striped brown head and a longer, more-pointed bill than the kingbird.

FOOD AND FORAGING

The Western Kingbird displays a typical flycatcher foraging behavior known as hawking: it watches for flying insects while perched, flies from the perch to capture the insect with a quick burst of speed, and then returns to the same perch. Westerns will also drop to the ground to capture prey and will pluck food items, such as insects and berries, from vegetation while hovering in the air.

PAIRING AND PARENTING

After pairing at their nesting grounds, a male and female search for nest sites near the tops of trees and shrubs or on human-made structures such as utility poles and abandoned buildings. The female constructs a bulky, cup-shaped nest and incubates an average of four eggs for two weeks. Pairs vigorously defend their conspicuous nests by dive-bombing potential predators while making loud calls and snapping their bills. Both parents capture insects to feed to their young during the 16-day nestling period.

MIGRATIONS AND MOVEMENTS

Western Kingbirds arrive in the Northwest in late April or early May and, after nesting, depart for wintering grounds by mid-September. They spend the winter in southern Mexico and Central America, mingling with other North American migrants and year-round tropical residents.

WHERE TO FIND WESTERN KINGBIRDS

This species is found in open country where perches such as scattered trees and transmission lines are available. They are much more commonly found east of the Cascades, but they do show up in pockets of appropriate habitat on the western side, especially during migration. Westerns act as if they want to be seen, so you won't have to wait long to find one if you're in the bird's habitat. Transmission lines and fences are favorite perches.

In Washington

Toppenish National Wildlife Refuge near Yakima

Marymoor Park in Redmond

Point No Point Lighthouse and County Park near Kingston

Wenas Basin between Yakima and Ellensburg

In Oregon

Sandy River Delta near Troutdale

Smith Rock State Park near Redmond

Klamath Falls area

North Mountain Park in Ashland

OTHER BIRDS TO SEE

While watching wires for Western Kingbirds, you might find other birds that enjoy a good view, such as American Kestrels, WESTERN MEADOWLARKS, Lark Sparrows, Loggerhead Shrikes, and WESTERN BLUEBIRDS.

VIOLET-GREEN SWALLOW

Tachycineta thalassina

SWOOPING ACROBATICALLY ABOVE the tree-tops like avian fighter pilots, Violet-green Swallows provide ray gun sound effects as they zoom past each other. They are harbingers of spring and the epitome of grace as they zip through the sky. These delicate, jewel-like birds will happily line up together on a telephone wire but will get feisty when limited nesting cavities are up for grabs.

Their iridescent green-and-violet back contrasts sharply with a pure white belly and chin. The only other northwestern swallow with a bright white belly and dark back is the Tree Swallow, which has a dark face and a metallic-blue back. Violet-greens have white flanks that wrap around and almost connect above the tail. When a Violet-green banks sharply, its white flanks stand out against its dark back and tail.

FOOD AND FORAGING

Like other swallows, Violet-greens eat flying insects and other drifting arthropods. They often fly above the treetops of coniferous forests, catching and swallowing insects in the air.

PAIRING AND PARENTING

Violet-greens nest in other bird-made cavities, such as those previously excavated by woodpeckers, or in nest boxes constructed by humans. Once a pair has settled on a suitable cavity, the female lines the space with twigs, grass, and feathers. Large white feathers are preferred, perhaps because they camouflage the white eggs from predators or from female swallows looking to dump an egg into another's clutch. Females incubate four to six eggs for 15 days, and both parents feed regurgitated insects to the nestlings.

MIGRATIONS AND MOVEMENTS

Although a migratory species, Violet-green Swallows spend much of the year in the Pacific Northwest. The northern extent of their wintering range is in central California, so some have a short migration and arrive at Northwest nesting sites as soon as late February. After the long nesting season, they gather in large flocks prior to migrating south. The last southbound flocks pass through our region in October.

WHERE TO FIND VIOLET-GREEN SWALLOWS

This species doesn't require an open, buggy wetland like many of its swallow cousins. Instead, it hunts insects over forests, along coastal areas, and in high-elevation areas. They are widespread across the Northwest and are excellent nest box tenants if you have them in your neighborhood. Swallows are often seen flying in the open and perching on wires. Spotting a swallow is easier than figuring out which species you're looking at.

OTHER BIRDS TO SEE

Aerial insects are an important food resource that is exploited by a variety of birds that either flutter like VAUX'S SWIFTS, swoop like Barn Swallows, or dart into the air and snatch like OLIVE-SIDED FLYCATCHERS and Pacific-slope Flycatchers.

WESTERN BLUEBIRD

Sialia mexicana

BLUEBIRDS ARE SYMBOLS of happiness for good reason. Their bright colors and fluttering flight will lift your mood at any time of the year. Their stubby beaks and small, dark eyes give them a cute appearance that, along with their willingness to use nest boxes, endears them to those who like their birds up close and adorable.

Male Western Bluebirds are glorious in deep blue plumage with a bold rufous (reddish) chest. Females are a grayed, washed out version of the same color scheme. Mountain Bluebirds sometimes are found in the same areas but are solid blue and lack the reddish coloration. Lazuli Buntings look similar, but they are a lighter, brighter blue and have white bars on their wings.

FOOD AND FORAGING

A Western Bluebird scans for insects from a tree branch or similar perch. When it sees an insect, usually on the ground, it pounces, captures the creature in its bill, and returns to another perch. Westerns also capture flying insects in the air and pluck food from vegetation while in flight. During the winter, they add fruit and seeds to their diet.

PAIRING AND PARENTING

Western Bluebirds typically nest in tree cavities that were previously excavated by woodpeckers in forests with widely spaced trees. They will also use nest boxes provided by bluebird enthusiasts. After a pair selects a nest site, the female fills much of the cavity or nest box with collected material such as dried grass and bark. She incubates an average of five eggs for about two weeks. Although the male does not incubate, he contributes to the nesting effort by feeding the female while she incubates and by helping her provision the young.

MIGRATIONS AND MOVEMENTS

With some moving short distances after nesting and some staying in an area year-round, Western Bluebirds are partial migrants. After the spring and summer nesting season, they form flocks that you can see throughout the winter in the western half of our region. In mild years, they can be found in Central Oregon and Washington as well.

WHERE TO FIND WESTERN BLUEBIRDS

Places such as Bickleton, Washington, and Champoeg, Oregon, where nest boxes have been erected along bluebird trails, make it almost too easy to find a Western Bluebird during nesting season. Less time searching for them means more time watching and enjoying them. This quiet bird lets its color do the talking, so you probably won't find it by listening for it. Watch for a flash of blue diving toward the ground from a fence post or the branch of a Ponderosa pine. Bluebirds are active creatures, so their movements will eventually catch your eye.

In Washington

Along the Goldendale-Bickleton Highway northeast of The Dalles, Oregon

Fort Simcoe State Park near Toppenish

Wenas Basin between Yakima and Ellensburg

Mima Mounds Natural Area Preserve near Olympia

Male (left) and female Western Bluebirds

In Oregon

Prescott Park in Medford

Champoeg State Heritage Area near Wilsonville

Ankeny National Wildlife Refuge near Albany

Baskett Slough National Wildlife Refuge near Dallas

William L. Finley National Wildlife Refuge near Corvallis

OTHER BIRDS TO SEE

The tiny town of Bickleton is considered the Bluebird Capital of Washington, and you'll see why as you drive the Goldendale-Bickleton Highway and visit the bluebird trails around town. In addition to the Western and MOUNTAIN BLUEBIRDS that nest in the abundant next boxes, you might find LEWIS'S WOODPECKERS, WESTERN TANAGERS, White-breasted Nuthatches, and Vesper Sparrows in the grasslands and trees.

MOUNTAIN BLUEBIRD

Sialia currucoides

LIKE POWDER BLUE jewels, Mountain Bluebirds brighten up the dry, open country of Central Oregon and Washington. In the winter, they look like a sliver of summer sky preserved to enjoy during the darker times. These long-winged beauties show off their good looks while perching conspicuously or hovering to find insects.

Males are a glorious sky blue all over, unlike other bluebirds. Females are grayer but still have the distinctive blue on their wings and tail. You can tell Mountain Bluebirds from Western Bluebirds by the reddish tones on the Western's chest. Pinyon Jays are a similar powder blue, but they are much larger and louder, with big beaks.

FOOD AND FORAGING

Owing to its affinity for open spaces, this relatively long-winged bluebird frequently hovers in place while searching for prey over bare ground or areas with short vegetation.

Mountain Bluebirds employ a variety of other methods to capture insects, including pouncing from a perch or darting from a perch to pursue flying insects. When insects are unavailable in the winter, the birds shift to a diet of fruit and seeds.

PAIRING AND PARENTING

Mountain Bluebirds historically depended on old woodpecker cavities in trees adjacent to open areas such as mountain meadows or wild-fire sites. Thanks to nest box programs, they now have less-specific habitat requirements. A female lines the inside of a cavity or nest box interior with dried grasses and pieces of bark before laying five or six eggs that she incubates for about two weeks. The male feeds the female while she incubates and joins her in capturing and delivering food to the nestlings. Young are dependent on their parents for several weeks after leaving the nest.

Female
Mountain
Bluebird

MIGRATIONS AND MOVEMENTS

Post-breeding flocks depart the Northwest for wintering grounds in the southwestern United States and northern Mexico by the end of Octo-ber. There, Mountain Bluebirds join mixed-species flocks until returning to the Northwest in late February and March. If the weather remains mild, some flocks will winter in Cen-tral Oregon and Washington.

WHERE TO FIND MOUNTAIN BLUEBIRDS

Don't let the name fool you, because these birds are found in flat, open valleys between moun-tain ranges in addition to their namesake alpine areas. They occur in areas that are more wide open than those favored by Western Bluebirds. Scan potential perches, such as fence lines and junipers, for a telltale blue flash. When hunting, Mountain Bluebirds hover low over fields, so don't look too high in sky.

In Washington

Along the Goldendale-Bickleton Highway
    northeast of The Dalles, Oregon

Wenas Basin between Yakima and Ellensburg

Coldwater Ridge Visitor Center on Mount Saint
    Helens

Mount Rainier National Park

In Oregon

Around Timberline Lodge on Mount Hood

Smith Rock State Park near Redmond

Davis Lake near La Pine

Crater Lake National Park

OTHER BIRDS TO SEE

High altitude, wildfires, and lava flows create forest openings that attract Mountain Blue-birds and more. An alpine hike can produce COMMON RAVENS, RED CROSSBILLS, BLACK-BACKED WOODPECKERS, Clark's Nutcrackers, and Gray Jays.

CEDAR WAXWING

Bombycilla cedrorum

A NOMADIC AND colorful fruit-eater, the Cedar Waxwing is striking as an individual or as a member of a busy flock setting a berry bush aquiver with fluttering wings and gaping mouths. These gluttonous and gregarious birds have a reputation for stripping fruit trees bare as they stuff themselves. In the fall, when ripened fruits have begun to ferment, some of them act suspiciously tipsy.

Cedar Waxwings have soft brown plumage that looks like sleek, short fur. The yellow edges of their tails will catch your eye, even when the birds are in flight. A very close look will reward you with a glimpse of the red waxy deposit on their wings that gives them their name. As small, brown birds with crests, they are distinctive in the Northwest. Their only look-alike is the Bohemian Waxwing, which is a winter visitor to the eastern parts of Oregon and Washington and is larger and grayer.

FOOD AND FORAGING

To meet their nutritional needs, Cedar Waxwings seem to imitate other birds. When fruits are abundant on wild plants or in berry farms, they pluck them from branches, hanging upside down like parakeets. When insects are on the menu, Cedar Waxwings emulate swallows, flycatchers, and warblers by catching prey on the wing or plucking them from vegetation.

PAIRING AND PARENTING

Pairs begin nesting in June, later than most songbirds. This delayed nesting season coincides nicely with the ripening of the local fruit crop, an important source of food for fledglings. Males and females collect nest material and bring it to a tree or large shrub, but the female performs most of the construction. Four eggs are incubated for 12 days. Nestlings are fed insects upon hatching, but the parents eventually transition them to a fruit-heavy diet.

MIGRATIONS AND MOVEMENTS

Flocks roam the countryside in search of productive fruit crops. They may leave the region in the fall or winter if fruit supplies are low, but they will return by the start of the nesting season in June.

WHERE TO FIND CEDAR WAXWINGS

Cedar Waxwings are most often spotted in deciduous woodlands, parks, and suburban areas. Forest edges with fruiting trees are prime locations for watching them. In town, look in holly and hawthorn trees during the winter, when they are full of red fruit and excited birds. The Cedar's call is very distinctive but is so high pitched that you may find it difficult to hear. Listen for the repeated, soft "seee" as a flock moves from one fruit tree to another.

OTHER BIRDS TO SEE

When the nesting season has ended, Cedar Waxwings diversify their diets to include a fall feast of berries. Joining them are American Robins, RED-BREASTED SAPSUCKERS, WESTERN BLUEBIRDS, and Western Scrub-Jays.

TOWNSEND'S WARBLER

Setophaga townsendi

AMID THE DRAB-BROWN wintering sparrows at your suet feeder comes a summery flash of hyperactive yellow, like a gigantic bumblebee. A visiting Townsend's Warbler will brighten your yard like few birds can. The beautifully marked yellow, black, and olive warblers stand out among their brown companions and delight birders with their energetic behavior.

You can distinguish warblers from other songbirds by their thin, pointed bills. No other warbler in the Northwest has the strong black and yellow facial striping of the Townsend's Warbler. Hermit Warblers have a solid yellow face, Wilson's Warblers have black only on top of their heads, and Common Yellowthroats have a thick black Zorro mask.

Male Townsend's Warbler

FOOD AND FORAGING

Typical of warblers, Townsend's seem to be constantly on the move when searching for food. They hop or fly from branch to branch while gleaning insects from coniferous and deciduous trees. These warblers also hover in place to pluck an insect off the tip of a twig, or they dart out to catch a meal in flight. During the winter, they will also pluck fruit and seeds from plants and pick at a suet feeder. This nonstop movement can make it difficult for the novice birder to spot the bird and identify it.

PAIRING AND PARENTING

Beginning in the late spring, the female constructs a bulky cup nest in a coniferous tree and incubates four or five eggs for 11 to 14 days, while the male keeps a close watch. Nestlings remain in the nest for only 10 days, probably to reduce predation risk, during which time they are fed insects by both parents.

MIGRATIONS AND MOVEMENTS

In most of their nesting range, Townsend's Warblers are neotropical migrants that spend their winters in Latin America. A portion of the population, however, spends its winters in western Washington, Oregon, and California after nesting in British Columbia. Northwest nesters arrive from their southern wintering grounds in April and May and depart the region in September. Wintering birds arrive in the western portions of Oregon and Washington in the fall and leave for their nesting grounds in late spring. In the winter, Townsend's join chickadees, kinglets, and creepers to form mixed feeding flocks and take advantage of the extra sets of eyes to watch for predators such as Sharp-shinned Hawks and Northern Pygmy Owls.

WHERE TO FIND TOWNSEND'S WARBLERS

Spring migration and winter are the easiest times to see these birds. In the summer, they are busy nesting in treetops in high-elevation areas. During spring migration in May, look for Townsend's Warblers in deciduous trees such as maples. In the winter, they favor conifers such as Douglas-firs. Their high foraging sites are responsible for a familiar birder's condition: warbler neck, an ache caused by tilting your head to stare up into a tree for long periods of time.

In Washington

Washington Park Arboretum in Seattle (winter)

Point Defiance Park in Tacoma (winter and migration)

Lake Wenatchee State Park near Leavenworth (breeding)

Mount Rainier National Park (breeding)

In Oregon

Mount Tabor Park in Portland (migration)

Jenkins Estate in Beaverton (winter)

Larch Mountain near Troutdale (breeding)

Fish Lake Interpretive Day Use Site near McKenzie Bridge (breeding)

OTHER BIRDS TO SEE

During the winter, conifer-filled urban parks provide shelter and feeding opportunities for birds such as RED-BREASTED SAPSUCKERS, BUSHTITS, RED-BREASTED NUTHATCHES, BROWN CREEPERS, ANNA'S HUMMINGBIRDS, and VARIED THRUSHES.

Female Townsend's Warbler

WILSON'S WARBLER

Cardellina pusilla

ON A RAINY spring day, the song and bright yellow flash of a Wilson's Warbler might be the only indication that summer is on its way. These warblers seem conflicted about whether they want to be seen: males announce their presence with a loud song and then disappear into the willows. Despite this contradiction, they are an ideal introductory warbler with their distinct field marks and eye-level lifestyle.

Males are bright yellow with an olive back and a jaunty black cap. Their black eyes stand out sharply against their yellow faces. The female's colors are more faded, and her cap is more olive than black. Almost all warblers have yellow on at least some part of their body, but the Wilson's is the only one with a yellow face and a dark cap.

FOOD AND FORAGING

Wilson's Warblers' hunting behavior makes them excellent birds to watch during migration or nesting time, because they often search for food near the ground, where you can catch a view more easily. They spend most of their time in deciduous trees or shrubs gleaning caterpillars and other insects from the foliage by hovering and pecking.

PAIRING AND PARENTING

Just as they forage low, Wilson's also nest at heights lower than most western warblers. Their nest is an open cup constructed in a shrub or in a depression on the ground near the trunk of a shrub or small tree. Three to five eggs are incubated for 11 days. Both parents feed insects and spiders to the young until they leave the nest 9 to 11 days after hatching.

Male
Wilson's
Warbler

MIGRATIONS AND MOVEMENTS

During spring migration in April and May, these birds appear to be everywhere as they forage like mad during the day to fuel up for their evening flights. After nesting here in the spring and summer, they depart the region by the end of October. The widespread population of Wilson's in the western United States migrates south to spend winters in a relatively small portion of western Mexico and Central America.

WHERE TO FIND WILSON'S WARBLERS

Look for them along rivers, in city parks, and in your own back yard. In early May, they seem to inhabit every shrub, but you can see and hear them all summer. Their song is not especially musical and sounds like an engine struggling to turn over, with a loud, rapid series of "chee" sounds. When you hear its song, look for a flash of yellow in a shrub or in the lower branches of a tree.

In Washington

Nisqually National Wildlife Refuge near Olympia

Magnuson Park in Seattle

Marymoor Park in Redmond

Wenatchee Confluence State Park in Wenatchee

In Oregon

Mary's Peak near Corvallis

Audubon Society of Portland's Nature Sanctuary near Forest Park

Tillamook Forest Center on Highway 6

Beaver Creek State Natural Area near Newport

OTHER BIRDS TO SEE

While you're staring into the bushes, you can enjoy spotting the other birds that hang out at eye level in riparian shrubs. Look for SWAINSON'S THRUSHES, Song Sparrows, PACIFIC WRENS, Spotted Towhees, and Downy Woodpeckers without straining your neck.

GREEN-TAILED TOWHEE

Pipilo chlorurus

DO NOT PASS up a chance to catch a glimpse of a singing male Green-tailed Towhee when you visit its Central Oregon habitat. Although males sing prominently like mockingbirds in the early summer, they seem to spend the rest of the year hiding from birders.

This large sparrow's sharp but earthy colors seem perfectly suited to its arid nesting grounds. It sports a rufous (reddish) cap, a white throat, and a unique olive-green color on its wings and tail. Males and females share this distinctive plumage pattern. Chipping Sparrows also have a rufous crown, but they are much smaller and are brown rather than green.

FOOD AND FORAGING

The Green-tailed and other towhees are masters of the hop-scratch, a foraging technique that involves hopping in the air and then scratching the ground with both feet simultaneously. This motion kicks litter out of the way so the birds can pick the insects or seeds off the ground. Green-taileds also search shrubs for insects and fruit.

PAIRING AND PARENTING

After selecting a nesting site in an area full of sagebrush, manzanita, or other shrubs and small trees, the female constructs the nest on the ground or in a shrub and lays three to four eggs. When alarmed, she hops off her nest and runs away instead of flying, making it difficult for predators such as squirrels, Common Ravens, and Steller's Jays to discern the nest's location. She incubates the eggs for 12 days, and both parents feed the nestlings until they leave the nest, 11 to 14 days after hatching.

MIGRATIONS AND MOVEMENTS

These short-distance migrants spend their winters in the southwestern United States and in Mexico. Nesting birds arrive in Oregon and Washington in late April or early May. After nesting, some birds move up in elevation to areas where more insects are available to fuel their molting and migration. Most leave the Northwest by the end of September.

WHERE TO FIND GREEN-TAILED TOWHEES

The range of the species in Washington is restricted to a small area in the extreme southeastern part of the state. In Oregon, they are much more widespread, nesting as far west as the Siskiyous and the eastern slopes of the Cascades. They prefer areas with a mix of shrubs and trees in dry and/or high country. Ideally, you will hear a male singing his variable song and then spot him on his low perch. If that fails, listen carefully for the rustling sound of a bird scratching in the leaf litter, and then track it down.

In Oregon

Cold Springs and Indian Ford campgrounds
near Sisters

Fort Rock State Park near La Pine

Davis Lake near La Pine

Cabin Lake Campground near Fort Rock

Mount Ashland near Ashland

OTHER BIRDS TO SEE

Brushy areas in the dry country are good places
to play What's behind that shrub? If it's not a
GREEN-TAILED TOWHEE, the answer could be
Fox Sparrow, Chipping Sparrow, CALIFORNIA
QUAIL, or a lizard.

WESTERN TANAGER

Piranga ludoviciana

Female
Western
Tanager

THE GODS OF biogeography were stingy with the Northwest, giving us only one tanager species. Fortunately for us, though, the Western Tanager is a vividly colored tropical ambassador that is easy to find during certain times of the year. The male's yellow body and red-orange head give it a pleasing resemblance to a fruity drink topped with a splash of grenadine.

The bold yellow body, red head, and black wings of the male Western Tanager have led many people to phone their local Audubon Society with questions about the parakeet or other exotic bird they think they have found in their yard. Females are less colorful, with an olive body, gray wings, and pale wing bars. Both sexes have a conical bill and are larger and chunkier than warblers.

FOOD AND FORAGING

Like many other neotropical migrants, Western Tanagers eat insects during the nesting season in the Pacific Northwest but switch to a diet heavy in fruit while wintering in Latin America. Bees, wasps, and ants make up a large part of the insect prey they capture. They search for insects in the high branches of trees or nab them in flight in a manner similar to that of flycatchers.

PAIRING AND PARENTING

Soon after a pair arrives on the nesting grounds, the female selects a nest site, usually 10 feet or higher in a coniferous tree. Nesting activity is difficult to observe in this species because of the height and concealment of its nest and the fact that the male, more colorful than the female, rarely visits the nest until the eggs hatch. The nest is saucer-shaped and lined with soft material. Four eggs are incubated for 13 days. Both parents feed the young during their 13-day nestling period.

MIGRATIONS AND MOVEMENTS

Westerns are highly migratory, meaning that all individuals leave their nesting grounds for southern wintering locales. The wintering grounds stretch from Southern California to Panama. Most springtime migrants enter the Northwest in late April or early May. After the nesting season, the last migrants have departed from the region by the end of October.

WHERE TO FIND WESTERN TANAGERS

You won't find many Western Tanagers in the middle of a shady old-growth forest; they prefer forest edges where conifers meet deciduous trees, rivers, or open space. This, and the bright plumage of the male, makes them easy to spot.

Male
Western
Tanager

If you are in the right type of forest at the right time of year, it won't be long until you see the yellow and black flash of a Western. If you get impatient, listen for its froglike "prit-dip?" call.

In Washington

Discovery Park in Seattle

Leavenworth National Fish Hatchery near Leavenworth

Oak Creek Wildlife Area near Naches

Nisqually National Wildlife Refuge near Olympia

In Oregon

Pittock Mansion in Portland

Mount Tabor Park in Portland

Willamette Park and Natural Area in Corvallis

Cooper Mountain Nature Park in Beaverton

Metolius Preserve and Metolius River trails near Camp Sherman

OTHER BIRDS TO SEE

Openings in the forest near meadows and streams attract a great diversity of birds and provide good visibility for finding them. A summertime stroll through the forest can lead you to WHITE-HEADED WOODPECKERS (east of the Cascade Crest), BLACK-HEADED GROSBEAKS, Western Wood-Pewees, Warbling Vireos, and Black-throated Gray Warblers.

LAZULI BUNTING

Passerina amoena

MALE LAZULI BUNTINGS sport electric-blue plumage and sing their little hearts out to impress the more modestly colored females. Their otherworldly color comes not from a blue pigment but from the light of the sun refracting in the structure of their feathers. In the shade, their color becomes dull. Visit a shrubby site in the late spring to take in their audiovisual show.

Males are boldly patterned, with a bright blue suit and rust-colored cummerbund. The color combination of blue and rufous is one that Lazuli Buntings share with Western Bluebirds. They are easily told apart, however, because the bunting has white wing bars and is a lighter blue, and the bluebird is larger and darker with a thinner bill. Female Lazulis are a warm brown with just a hint of blue on the wing.

Female Lazuli Bunting

FOOD AND FORAGING

Lazulis have a very flexible diet and foraging strategy. They use their thick bills to crunch seeds that they find on the ground or remove from plants. They also pick berries from shrubs or trees, pull tent caterpillars from their webs, and capture flying insects in the air.

PAIRING AND PARENTING

Male Lazulis sing persistently at their nesting grounds to attract females. No two songs sound the same, because each young male crafts his song by incorporating phrases sung by older neighbors. After pairing, females construct a nest a few feet off the ground in a shrub or small tree. Three or four eggs are incubated for 12 days. Both parents feed insects and spiders to the nestlings until they fledge, 10 days after hatching. Males attempt to nest during their first breeding season but won't grow their electric blue plumage until the following year.

MIGRATIONS AND MOVEMENTS

Most Lazulis arrive to nest in Oregon and Washington in May and leave the region by the end of August. On their way to their wintering grounds in Mexico, some birds make a pit stop in the southwestern United States to molt, or shed and regrow their feathers. Once the molt is complete, the buntings complete their migration.

Male
Lazuli
Bunting

WHERE TO FIND LAZULI BUNTINGS

Look for this species in habitats ranging from grassy savannahs to riparian willow thickets, but shrubs for nesting and some sort of singing perches are always needed. Springtime is when the males are most visible, and they shine like pieces of aquamarine in the sun while performing. Check the tops of shrubs and small trees to catch a great view of a male in his sunlit splendor.

In Washington

Cowiche Canyon near Yakima

Toppenish National Wildlife Refuge near Yakima

Steigerwald Lake National Wildlife Refuge near Washougal

Howard Miller Steelhead Park near Rockport

In Oregon

Powell Butte Nature Park in Portland

Sandy River Delta near Troutdale

Hagelstein Park near Klamath Falls

Mount Ashland near Ashland

OTHER BIRDS TO SEE

Shrubby hillsides are full of birds on the ground, on perches, and flying overhead. You might find Savannah Sparrows, Common Yellowthroats, American Goldfinches, WESTERN BLUEBIRDS, and VIOLET-GREEN SWALLOWS.

YELLOW-HEADED BLACKBIRD

Xanthocephalus xanthocephalus

Female
Yellow-headed
Blackbird

AS WE WATCH Red-winged Blackbirds in winter, we can't help but wonder, how long until the Yellow-headed Blackbirds return? These big, brash birds are the life of the party in marshes across the Northwest every summer. The male takes every opportunity to puff up and sing his unmusical, some say laughable, song to charm the harem of females that nest in his territory.

Nothing else looks like the aptly named Yellow-headed Blackbird; even the females have yellow throats and breasts. The male's white wing patch makes him even more eye-catching. Other blackbirds have black heads and may show a colored shoulder patch, or epaulette.

FOOD AND FORAGING

Yellow-headed Blackbirds eat cultivated grains and wild seeds throughout much of the year, but they switch to a diet of emergent aquatic insects, especially dragonflies, during the nesting season. When not occupying their marshy nesting sites, large flocks of these birds walk through agricultural fields, scouring the ground for insects and unharvested grain.

PAIRING AND PARENTING

Males establish territories in freshwater marshes with deep water and vegetation, such as cattails, available for nest building. After excluding smaller Red-winged Blackbirds to the outer fringes of the marsh, a Yellow-headed male will attract up to eight females with which to breed. Each female weaves a basket-like nest into cattails or other aquatic plants within the male's territory. She incubates her eggs for 12 to 13 days while the male vigilantly guards the territory from intruders. The female feeds dragonflies and other insects to the nestlings, and the male may help with the feeding, depending on the number of nests he fathered. Nestlings leave the nest about 10 days after hatching and eventually join flocks with others of the same species.

MIGRATIONS AND MOVEMENTS

Some Yellow-headed Blackbirds winter in the Northwest, but most travel to wintering grounds in the southern United States and Mexico. Flocks return to the region in April for

Male
Yellow-headed
Blackbird

nesting season, which generally lasts from May through August. Birds that travel south depart by the end of September.

WHERE TO FIND YELLOW-HEADED BLACKBIRDS

Although they are more widespread on the east side of the Cascades, Yellow-headed Blackbirds are found at a few west side sites as well. Their hunger for dragonflies attracts them to large, deep marshes and ponds with plenty of cattails for perching and nest-building. The combination of its bright-yellow head and braying song ensures that you won't miss this blackbird in the spring or early summer. Males often sing from cattails or other exposed perches, and in some places they cover the fences and roadsides, making them difficult to ignore—not that you'd want to.

In Washington

Toppenish National Wildlife Refuge near Yakima

Ridgefield National Wildlife Refuge near Vancouver

Nisqually National Wildlife Refuge near Olympia

Conboy Lake National Wildlife Refuge near Glenwood

In Oregon

Klamath Marsh National Wildlife Refuge near Klamath Falls

Vanport Wetlands in Portland

Fern Ridge Wildlife Management Area near Eugene

Hatfield Lake near Bend

OTHER BIRDS TO SEE

Wetlands are bustling with bird activity during the nesting season. Marsh Wrens build bulky nests in cattails, Tree Swallows fight over nest boxes, AMERICAN BITTERNS make their booming calls from deep in the grass, and CINNAMON TEALS flash their turquoise wing patches as they rocket from the water.

RED CROSSBILL

Loxia curvirostra

THE CHALLENGE OF extracting tiny seeds from a cone has led to the evolution of a truly bizarre crossed beak. Although its bill looks deformed, the Red Crossbill is actually armed with a perfect cone-opening apparatus and is ideally suited to a life feasting on treetop conifer seeds. Parrotlike in their behavior, crossbills hang upside down to grab every last cone and squabble loudly with their flock mates over who gets first dibs at the feeder.

Males are red and females are yellow, and young males can be a blotchy mix between the two. White-winged Crossbills are rarer than Red Crossbills and have conspicuous white wing patches, as their name suggests. House,

Purple, and Cassin's finches, although also reddish colored seed-eaters, have uncrossed beaks, are slimmer, and are less red than Red Crossbills.

FOOD AND FORAGING

Red Crossbills are extremely specialized seed-eaters. When feeding, they fly into and climb trees to reach cones. A crossbill bites into a cone, moves the lower portion of its bill sideways to spread the cone's scales, and then sticks its tongue into the cone to pull out the seed. This process is repeated thousands of times by a flock until most of the seeds in a tree are consumed. Although conifer seeds make up the bulk of their diet, Red Crossbills also eat the buds of deciduous trees such as alders, seed provided at bird feeders, and, occasionally, insects such as aphids found on cone-bearing trees.

PAIRING AND PARENTING

Male Red Crossbill

Breeding begins wherever and whenever a good cone crop is available, from December to September, with crossbills taking a break from breeding in the fall to molt. In a productive cone year, pairs can successfully raise up to four broods of young. The female constructs a nest of small twigs lined with fine plant material and feathers. Three eggs are incubated for 14 days. Both parents feed the nestlings a regurgitated slurry of mashed seeds, saliva, and possibly insects. The amount of time nestlings spend in the nest depends on the quality of the food supply and ranges from 15 to 35 days. Fledglings' bills are not fully crossed when they leave the nest, so they are dependent on their parents for food until they develop the tools and skills to open cones for themselves.

MIGRATIONS AND MOVEMENTS

The timing of cone production by coniferous trees forces Red Crossbills to live a nomadic existence in search of cone crops, the quantity of which varies from year to year. Crossbills stay in the Pacific Northwest throughout the year, but their presence at a particular time and location is never guaranteed.

WHERE TO FIND RED CROSSBILLS

Summer is the most likely time to find crossbills on either side of the Cascade Crest. If you find a flock in the winter, you could be rewarded with the sight of dozens of them decorating a tree like red and yellow ornaments. If you don't see them, you can often locate them by following the sound of their flight call, a distinctive "pip-pip-pip."

In Washington

Cape Disappointment State Park near Ilwaco

Wenas Campground (Audubon Campground) near Ellensburg (rough road)

Restoration Point on Bainbridge Island

Discovery Park in Seattle

In Oregon

Cold Springs Campground near Sisters

Ecola State Park near Cannon Beach

Larch Mountain near Troutdale

Crater Lake National Park

OTHER BIRDS TO SEE

In coniferous forests and adjoining clear-cut areas, you'll find BAND-TAILED PIGEONS, SWAINSON'S THRUSHES, Sooty Grouse, and MacGillivray's Warblers.

EVENING GROSBEAK

Coccothraustes vespertinus

Female Evening Grosbeak

EVENING GROSBEAKS ARE like Easter candy: in the spring they are everywhere you look, but in other times of year you can't find any no matter how hard you try. They are rare and gorgeous enough to be a special guest at a backyard feeder, at least until a marauding mob of them blows your seed budget.

Males look dashing in their smooth yellow plumage that fades to a dark head. Their thick yellow eyebrow stripe and black-and-white wings make them stand out, even in flight. Females are a grayer version of the males. Evening Grosbeaks are much chunkier and have much thicker beaks than either of the goldfinches that share their yellow coloration.

FOOD AND FORAGING

This bird's oversized bill is powerful enough to crack a cherry seed, which it swallows after removing the skin and flesh. Evening Grosbeaks search for food in trees, frequently in flocks. In addition to cherries, they eat maple seeds, leaf buds, insects, and seeds from cones of coniferous trees.

PAIRING AND PARENTING

Unlike that of other songbirds, the courtship characteristics of Evening Grosbeaks are quite understated. The male rarely sings and lets his striking plumage attract the female's attention. The female builds a simple platform of a nest at least 10 feet up in a tree. Three or four eggs are incubated for 13 days. In many places, the nesting season is timed so that caterpillar emergence coincides with the nesting period. Both parents feed regurgitated caterpillars to the newly hatched young and deliver whole caterpillars to older nestlings that leave the nest two weeks after hatching.

MIGRATIONS AND MOVEMENTS

Evening Grosbeaks may be seen year-round in the Northwest, with an emphasis on "may." When food supplies, such as seed-bearing cones, are exhausted in the fall or winter, they travel far from their usual ranges to find other types of food. They are most frequently observed in lowland valleys and coastal areas in the spring, but they seem to disappear in the summer when they are quietly nesting in mid- to high-elevation forests. They are abundant in lowland cities and towns during some winters, but they are absent in others.

WHERE TO FIND EVENING GROSBEAKS

Springtime is the best time to find Evening Grosbeaks. It seems that in every park you visit, a few are perched on the top of a conifer tree. During the winter, though, it's feast or famine, with 20 Evening Grosbeaks emptying your feeder one week and then none for

Male Evening
Grosbeak

months. Males will get your attention with their bright yellow plumage and their habit of calling repeatedly from the top of a tree. Individuals also call when flying. Their piercing call resembles the sound a child makes when pretending to shoot a laser gun: "tchoo, tchoo."

In Washington

Howard Miller Steelhead Park near Rockport

Blackbird Island in Leavenworth

Trout Lake Natural Area Preserve near Trout Lake

Discovery Park in Seattle

In Oregon

Pittock Mansion in Portland

Scoggins Valley Park near Forest Grove

Mary's Peak near Corvallis

Cooper Mountain Nature Park in Beaverton

OTHER BIRDS TO SEE

Fellow springtime migrants such as WESTERN TANAGERS, RUFOUS HUMMINGBIRDS, and TOWNSEND'S WARBLERS are also highly visible and abundant in late spring.

Fish-eating Birds
DIVING, PADDLING, AND STABBING TO CATCH SWIMMING PREY

AS A GENERAL RULE, a surefire way to find wildlife is to visit a body of water. Luckily for birders in the Northwest, the region offers rivers, bays, creeks, sloughs, lakes, sounds, straits, and of course the Pacific Ocean. These features shape the character of our region in many ways, not the least of which is through the presence of fish. This resource is pursued by a variety of predators, including some of the most highly specialized birds discussed in this book.

Fish-eating birds use their bills, their feet, and their wits to feed themselves from the waters that surround us. They all possess the quickness and visual acuity necessary to seize a wary meal from the water. Some eat virtually nothing but fish. For others, fish are part of a diet that also includes aquatic insects, crayfish, and mollusks.

Whatever the particulars of their diet might be, these birds are critically linked to the presence of clean water that supports healthy plant and animal communities. So when you hear the song of an American Dipper or view the dance of a Western Grebe, remember that, in response to a growing human population, conservation of water and habitat is necessary to protect the waterways and water birds of the western United States.

American
Bittern

HOODED MERGANSER

Lophodytes cucullatus

Male Hooded Merganser

AS THE MALE Hooded Merganser raises and lowers his showy feathered crest, he seems to be communicating in semaphore. Unlike the noisy Mallards and wigeons, Hooded Mergansers are not loquacious ducks—they let their appearance do the talking. Despite their flashy plumage, however, these birds can hide in plain sight by holding still against the far bank of a pond. They glide slowly and quietly between lily pads, nervously watching for danger with alert yellow eyes.

Males are boldly decorated birds with clean lines that look like they were painted with a broad brush. They are mostly black with a white chest and warm brown flanks. Their most prominent feature is a collapsible black crest with a large white patch, which gives their heads the shape of a hatchet blade. They can flatten their crest so the white patch is barely visible or raise it completely in what can only be a bid for attention. Females are drab gray with a smaller brown crest. Buffleheads and Surf Scoters also have large white patches on their heads, but their patches wrap around the backs of their heads, unlike the Hooded Merganser's patch, which is on the side of the head.

FOOD AND FORAGING

These diving ducks have a taste for aquatic animals. They pursue their prey under water, propelling themselves with their webbed feet. Using its excellent underwater eyesight and serrated bill, a diving Hooded Merganser captures fish, crayfish, insects, and mollusks.

PAIRING AND PARENTING

One of several duck species that nests in tree cavities or nest boxes, Hooded Mergansers place their nests at least 8 feet up and above or in sight of water. Like other ducks, the female plucks her own downy feathers to line her nest. She incubates 9 to 13 eggs for 33 days and cares for the ping-pong-ball–shaped eggs and fuzzy ducklings on her own. A day after hatching, ducklings must scale the vertical wall of their cavity or nest box, jump from the entrance, and find their mother, who will guide them to aquatic insects, which they are capable of capturing on their own.

MIGRATIONS AND MOVEMENTS

The species breeds in the Pacific Northwest starting in February or March, but they are more easily spotted in winter, when the region is full of migrants that have arrived from colder areas to the north and east. Upon reaching wintering grounds, small flocks form, and pairs that separated at the start of nesting may reunite. Northwest-nesting birds begin breeding before wintering birds depart for their nesting grounds.

WHERE TO FIND HOODED MERGANSERS

Hooded Mergansers are widespread in the wetter parts of the Pacific Northwest. Some hide in the vegetation along the edges of ponds and lakes, but others swim several yards from shore in large bays. The drab, brown females can easily escape notice by hiding in the shadows. Scan the water for the telltale flash of white in the male's crest that will likely lead you to the pair.

In Washington

Capitol Lake in Olympia

Union Bay Natural Area (Montlake Fill) in Seattle

Crockett Lake on Whidbey Island

Ridgefield National Wildlife Refuge near Vancouver

In Oregon

Koll Center Wetlands Park in Beaverton

Ankeny National Wildlife Refuge near Albany

Eckman Lake near Waldport

William L. Finley National Wildlife Refuge near Corvallis

OTHER BIRDS TO SEE

Hooded Mergansers are gorgeous birds that you can often see without even leaving town. They are frequent residents of urban and suburban parks and are much more visible and less secretive in the wintertime. Sharing city wetlands with Hooded Mergansers may be BELTED KINGFISHERS, GREAT BLUE HERONS, WOOD DUCKS, Ring-necked Ducks, Green-winged Teals, Common Mergansers, and Pied-billed Grebes.

Female Hooded Merganser

WESTERN GREBE

Aechmophorus occidentalis

A WESTERN GREBE glides across a lake like a low-slung Viking ship with a deadly sharp figurehead. Elegant and proud in its posture, it silently preens and prepares for its dancing debut. When it finds an appropriate partner, it exchanges dignity for exuberance and lets forth with moves that would put the finest synchronized swimmers to shame.

Western Grebes and their sister species, the Clark's Grebe, are the only black-and-white grebes with long necks. Distinguishing Westerns from smaller grebes is a cinch, but you need to look a little more closely to tell the Western and Clark's apart. Western Grebes have olive-green to yellow bills, and Clark's Grebes' bills are yellow-orange like a school bus. During the breeding season, and to some extent in the winter, Clark's show much more white on the face, including the area around their red eyes. Westerns have black feathers around their eyes. The flanks of the Clark's also show white feathers that Westerns lack.

FOOD AND FORAGING

With their long, incredibly thin necks, it seems impossible that Western Grebes could swallow anything larger than a noodle, but they are expert fish-eaters. While swimming at the surface, they dunk their head under water to find prey. To capture fish, they dive below the surface, propelling themselves with their lobed, not webbed, feet. They use their needlelike bills as a spear or a pair of forceps with which to capture fish, depending on the size of their prey. As with other grebes, Westerns have the peculiar habit of swallowing their own feathers when they are naturally shed. Scientists aren't sure why, but these feathers might protect the digestive tract from fish bones, might form pellets for regurgitation, or might shield the bird's intestines from parasites.

PAIRING AND PARENTING

The physics-defying courtship displays of Western Grebes must be seen to be believed. Displays include a rushing behavior, in which pairs run across the surface of the water in perfect synchrony, producing a loud pattering sound with their feet. Later on, pairs perform another ceremony that involves stretching their necks, diving for vegetation, and then standing on the surface of the water, bringing their bills full of weeds together until one tosses them aside. Western Grebes are so aquatically oriented that they don't even take to land to nest. Pairs make their nests on mats of aquatic vegetation in lakes, where three or four eggs are incubated for 24 days. Young grebes leave the nest and travel around the lake on their parents' backs just minutes after hatching. They continue to ride their parents' backs for two to four weeks and are fully independent when they are six or seven weeks old.

MIGRATIONS AND MOVEMENTS

Western Grebes arrive at inland breeding sites in March, and by May the courtship rituals are underway. Instead of flying south in the fall, they migrate westward to coastal areas at the end of the summer nesting season. From November through May, look for them swimming in ponds, lakes, bays, and the Pacific Ocean.

WHERE TO FIND WESTERN GREBES

Lakes on the east side of the Cascades are the best place to see dancing and breeding Western Grebes. In the winter, they gather in large numbers in coastal areas. They are often easy to spot because they prefer open, deep water for diving. Their contrasting black-and-white plumage also draws the eye.

In Washington

Dungeness National Wildlife Refuge near Sequim (winter)

Manchester State Park near Port Orchard (winter)

Alki Beach in West Seattle (winter)

Damon Point State Park in Ocean Shores (winter)

In Oregon

Hatfield Marine Science Center trail in Newport (winter)

Siuslaw River, South Jetty, near Florence (winter)

Coos Bay (winter)

Link River Trail in Klamath Falls (breeding)

OTHER BIRDS TO SEE

While visiting a lake to see dancing grebes, you might also see AMERICAN WHITE PELICANS, CASPIAN TERNS, and OSPREYS doing some fishing. RUDDY DUCKS and YELLOW-HEADED BLACKBIRDS provide colorful scenery in their breeding plumages.

AMERICAN BITTERN

Botaurus lentiginosus

WHILE BIRDING IN a wetland, you might hear a strange sound, as if a large bubble of gas has just risen to the top of the water. You aren't crazy. That low "ga-LUMP" is the call of an American Bittern, and sometimes that telltale weird noise is the only sign of one. If it feels nervous, this bird will either slink away through the grass without being detected or stand with its neck extended and bill pointed to the sky, its strongly striped white-and-brown neck resembling another bunch of grass stems. Even with its beak upraised, it can stare straight ahead to watch for danger. A sighting of this elusive bird is always a victory, because its sneaky ways make it a challenge.

American Bitterns are squatty birds with much shorter necks and legs than their relative, the Great Blue Heron. Green Herons and Night-Herons are also short, but both lack the warm brown coloring of the American Bittern and its defined neck stripes.

FOOD AND FORAGING

American Bitterns consume fish and a variety of other animals including insects, frogs, and snakes. They use stealthy moves and camouflage to sneak up on wetland prey. While holding its head horizontal, and seemingly staring forward, this bird can see into the water in which it is wading using its downward-pointed eyes.

PAIRING AND PARENTING

This bird constructs its nest on or near the ground in areas surrounded by dense wetland vegetation. Males vigorously defend breeding territories but do not provide parental care, leaving the incubating and feeding duties to the female. Three to five eggs are incubated for 24 to 28 days. Young leave the nest at one or two weeks of age but remain in the vicinity until they are old enough to fly.

MIGRATIONS AND MOVEMENTS

Look for American Bitterns throughout the year in western portions of Oregon and Washington. Males begin defending territories in March or April, and females construct nests as soon as the wetland vegetation has grown thick enough to provide some cover. After the nesting season, they spend the year in their nesting grounds if temperatures remain above freezing. In colder years, they migrate to warmer places.

WHERE TO FIND AMERICAN BITTERNS

Look for American Bitterns in marshy areas with lots of tall grass in which to hide. The national wildlife refuges of the Pacific Northwest provide this type of habitat in abundance and are a good place to start your search. Spring is the best time to spot the species because the grass is not tall enough to obscure the birds completely. They are experts at camouflage and at creeping around without moving a grass blade. Your best bet is to scan the edges of open marshy areas looking out for their pointed heads. Listen for their "ga-LUMP" call. This sound is so low in pitch that it you sometimes feel it more than hear it. You might be able to use the sound to narrow your search area. If you are lucky, you will see one flying silently from one area of dense vegetation to another.

In Washington

Ridgefield National Wildlife Refuge near
   Vancouver

Toppenish National Wildlife Refuge near
   Yakima

Steigerwald Lake National Wildlife Refuge near Washougal

Kent Ponds in the Green River Natural Resources Area near Seattle

In Oregon

Killin Wetlands near Banks

William L. Finley National Wildlife Refuge near Corvallis

Fern Ridge Wildlife Management Area near Eugene

Klamath Marsh National Wildlife Refuge near Klamath Falls

OTHER BIRDS TO SEE

In the early summer, wildlife refuges are alive with color and sound. Look for Common Yellowthroats, CEDAR WAXWINGS, GREEN HERONS, Tree Swallows, RED-TAILED HAWKS, Cinnamon Teals, Marsh Wrens, BLACK-HEADED GROSBEAKS, and Virginia Rails.

GREEN HERON

Butorides virescens

SOME BIRDS WOULD happily gulp down a crust of bread if you gave them one—gulls, for example. A Green Heron might pick up the crust, but it has other plans. It places the bit of food on the surface of the water below its perch and crouches, perfectly still, as it waits. Like any good angler, the bird repositions its lure when it drifts out of place. Finally, a small fish comes up to investigate the delicious morsel and is quickly grabbed and swallowed. No catch and release here.

Green Heron is a misnomer for a bird with a brick-red neck and dark gray-green wings. Its

stumpy legs are bright yellow, and white stripes appear on its chest. The overall impression is that of a dark, squat little heron that has no neck at all in most postures. When it stretches out to grab a fish, however, its whole silhouette changes, and suddenly its neck is longer than the rest of its body.

FOOD AND FORAGING

Unlike other herons, this species spends little time wading. It lacks the Great Blue's long legs and neck, which it needs to catch fish in deep water. Instead, a Green Heron lurks along the water's edge, waiting for an opportunity to grab a fish or aquatic invertebrate. Like human fish-seekers, the Green Heron gets creative by using bait—bits of vegetation, feathers, or other objects used to lure fish into striking distance. When fish approach, the bird captures them by spearing with its bill or diving after them. This unique behavior includes Green Herons in a small, elite group of nonhuman tool users.

PAIRING AND PARENTING

Nest sites can vary greatly: near the ground, high in a tree, along a river, in a wetland, on dry land with water in sight, and alone or in a colony of other water birds. Both parents incubate the three to five eggs for 20 days, and both provide food to the nestlings. Newly hatched young are fed partially digested food and later move on to intact prey. The young leave the nest 16 days after hatching, but they remain flightless and dependent on their parents for several more weeks.

MIGRATIONS AND MOVEMENTS

In the Pacific Northwest, most Green Herons nest during the summer months. They migrate to the southern United States or Latin America in August or September and return to the Northwest in April. Some individuals are observed throughout the winter in mild portions of western Oregon and western Washington, but in smaller numbers relative to spring and summer.

WHERE TO FIND GREEN HERONS

Green Herons occur regularly only on the west side of the Cascades. They are usually found in places with slow-moving or still water with overhanging vegetation. A tangle of willows on the edge of a pond is a good place to look. Diversion dams and small water control structures also make great perches. Scan the edge of the pond for the bump on a log that has a beak. You might also spot one as it flies away from you and gives a harsh "skow" call.

In Washington

Juanita Bay Park in Kirkland

Lake Sammamish State Park near Issaquah

Nisqually National Wildlife Refuge near Olympia

In Oregon

Oaks Bottom Wildlife Refuge in Portland

Tualatin River National Wildlife Refuge near Sherwood

North Mountain Park in Ashland

OTHER BIRDS TO SEE

As you search the water's edge for a Green Heron, look for other riparian birds such as BELTED KINGFISHERS, WOOD DUCKS, Red-winged Blackbirds, and WILSON'S WARBLERS.

OSPREY
Pandion haliaetus

IF OSPREYS SEEM a little more casual, a little less serious, than your average bird of prey, maybe it's because they can afford to be. They have a very high success rate when it comes to fishing, so they aren't worried about finding their next meal. Their disheveled head feathers give them a slightly goofy appearance, and their dives seem more exuberant than merely functional. It's difficult to say with birds, but they look like they are having fun.

Ospreys have a unique silhouette in flight that distinguishes them from all other birds of prey. Their long wings always have a crook in them that you won't find on hawks or eagles. When they are soaring above you, notice their mostly white body with dark patches on the wrists of their wings. If you get a close look at a perched Osprey, you'll see a dark line of feathers through the eye and a white stripe over it. Although its facial pattern might superficially resemble that of a young Bald Eagle, the Osprey weighs less than half as much, has gray feet instead of yellow, and its plumage is much less mottled.

FOOD AND FORAGING

Ospreys have a diving style that is unique in the world of fish-eaters. They will go after fish that are 12 inches or more under water, so they don't just scoop with their talons like a Bald Eagle. Instead, an Osprey becomes a dart by extending its feet downward, leaning its head forward over its ankles, and sweeping back its wings. It plunges into the water feet and headfirst and grabs the fish with its talons. After a successful dive, an Osprey uses its strong flight muscles to lift its soaked body and the heavy fish out of the water. Once airborne, it flies to a nest or perch with the fish facing forward in its talons.

PAIRING AND PARENTING

Pairs build large, conspicuous stick nests on a variety of man-made structures, in trees, and on cliffs. Nests are usually smaller than those of Bald Eagles and often contain decorations such as orange bailing twine. The male brings sticks to the female throughout the nesting season, and she arranges them on the nest. The female lays two to four eggs and performs most of the incubation. After the eggs hatch in 35 to 40 days, she leaves the fishing up to the male, who delivers fish for her to share with the young. Nestlings remain in the nest for at least 50 days after hatching and continue to be fed by their parents for several more weeks. The female migrates south by herself, leaving the male to continue caring for the young. After all the young have gone, the male finally heads south himself.

MIGRATIONS AND MOVEMENTS

The Osprey is a migratory bird whose movements have been well studied. At the end of the summer nesting season, they leave the Pacific Northwest for Mexico and Central America, a journey that lasts 10 to 20 days. Although Ospreys have strong pair bonds, males and females spend the migration and winter periods apart. After making their first southward migration, most of the young spend more than a year in the southern wintering grounds before returning north to mate for the first time. Ospreys are an early harbinger of spring in the Pacific Northwest, with established pairs reuniting at their nest sites in February and March.

WHERE TO FIND OSPREYS

Ospreys are widespread across the Pacific Northwest wherever they can find a combination of big water for fishing and trees or platforms for roosting and nesting. They are often seen soaring or hovering in place high above the water, looking for fish. Their nests are easy to find, because they favor the bare tops of trees as well as power poles and man-made nesting platforms.

In Washington

Leavenworth National Fish Hatchery near
    Leavenworth

North View and South View Parks on Port
    Gardner in Everett

Julia Butler Hansen Refuge near Cathlamet

Steigerwald Lake National Wildlife Refuge
    near Washougal

In Oregon

Multnomah Falls near Troutdale

Ankeny National Wildlife Refuge near Albany

Oaks Bottom Wildlife Refuge in Portland

Sauvie Island near Portland

OTHER BIRDS TO SEE

The Columbia Gorge can be windy in summer, but it's a great place to find nesting Ospreys as well as BALD EAGLES, AMERICAN DIPPERS, HARLEQUIN DUCKS, Double-crested Cormorants, and VIOLET-GREEN SWALLOWS.

CASPIAN TERN

Hydroprogne caspia

IF GULLS ARE too pushy for you, if you prefer a bird that doesn't eat French fries with such gusto, you can try the gulls' more business-like cousins: the terns. You won't find the Caspian Tern loitering in a strip mall parking lot. It spends its days flying over the water looking for fish, its black cap covering its eyes and giving it a serious expression. When Caspians call out to one another with their hoarse voices, they sound as though they are giving status reports. Sometimes they stop to rest on a sandbar, but they still look like they are contemplating the work that remains to be done.

Caspian Terns are the largest terns in the world, the size of a big gull, although their slender gray wings and graceful flight make them appear smaller. They have a black cap and a large, pointed, red-orange beak. The only other tern with black legs and a solid orange bill found in the Northwest is the Elegant Tern, which has a thin, drooping bill.

FOOD AND FORAGING

A Caspian Tern hunts fish on the wing, circling or hovering above a body of water with its face pointing downward. When it spots a fish, it dives into the water headfirst, catching the fish in its long bill. Its diet is variable and reflects the types of small fish present in the area.

PAIRING AND PARENTING

This species historically nested in small colonies or among colonies of other birds, such as gulls. Big changes in its nesting biology occurred in the 1980s, when large colonies of Caspian Terns formed near the mouth of the Columbia River to nest on islands created from dredged material. The mouth of the Columbia is made even more attractive by the large numbers of juvenile salmon and steelhead released by upstream hatcheries.

In their island colonies, Caspians lay two or three eggs in a shallow depression. Both parents incubate eggs for 27 days and feed fish to nestlings, which swallow fish whole. As young

Caspians grow, so does the size of fish delivered. Chicks can stand and leave the nest after several days, but they are dependent on their parents for food for several months. Adults continue caring for the young during post-breeding migration and teach them to fish by dropping food into the water.

MIGRATIONS AND MOVEMENTS

Caspian Terns wander widely after nesting. They begin their southward migration in late July and eventually follow the coast south to wintering grounds that stretch from California to South America. In spring, migration from wintering to nesting sites is more direct, with birds arriving in the Pacific Northwest from March to May. Nonbreeding Caspians search for fish along the coasts and large rivers of our region throughout the summer months.

WHERE TO FIND CASPIAN TERNS

The best time to find Caspian Terns in the Pacific Northwest is during the nesting season. The current center of their breeding abundance is East Sand Island near the mouth of the Columbia River, although they have been quick to abandon nest colonies where they are unsuccessful at raising chicks. They can also be seen traveling along the ocean shore, in the Salish Sea, at inland lakes, and along the Upper Columbia River. Sandy spits at the mouths of bays are common resting places. Caspians can often be spotted in flight along the shoreline or diving headfirst into bodies of water to catch fish. Listen for their hoarse calls.

OTHER BIRDS TO SEE

The mouth of the Columbia River is a real hotspot for Caspian Terns. A visit here in the summer might also produce BROWN PELICANS, nesting BRANDT'S CORMORANTS and PIGEON GUILLEMOTS, and glimpses of SOOTY SHEARWATERS FLYING by out past the jetties.

BELTED KINGFISHER

Megaceryle alcyon

Male Belted Kingfisher

WHO NEEDS THE circus when you can watch Belted Kingfishers put on their attention-grabbing show? The performers are dressed to entertain in blue suits and cummerbunds. Their head feathers are spiky pompadours, and their long beaks look like comedic props. When the show begins, you'll see high-speed chases, daring headfirst dives, and displays of fish-grabbing prowess, all to the soundtrack of their loud chattering. It's difficult to get too excited about mellower birds after you've seen the Theater of the Kingfisher.

With its big head, spiky crest, and oversized bill, this bird is unmistakable. Its slate-blue color and noisy rattling call further distinguish it from any similar birds. Although all Belted Kingfishers show the same bluish color on their back, you can distinguish between males, females, and juveniles if you view them from the front. All have a blue breast band, but females have a second rufous (reddish) band below it, and juveniles' rufous spurs don't extend to the front of their breasts.

FOOD AND FORAGING

Belted Kingfishers spend much of their time perched along the edges of streams, lakes, and bays watching for fish and other prey. They also hover in place with rapid wing beats while looking down into the water. When they spot a meal, they dive beak first and smack the water, but they rarely plunge their body below the surface. After a successful catch, Belted Kingfishers carry their fish to a perch, stun it by beating it against the perch, and then swallow it whole, headfirst.

PAIRING AND PARENTING

This species' nest is unique among the region's fish-eating birds. Pairs work together to excavate a horizontal burrow into the exposed soil of a riverbank. Both parents enter the nesting chamber to incubate the six or seven eggs and feed nestlings that hatch in 22 days. On the menu for newly hatched nestlings: regurgitated balls of partially digested fish. As nestlings grow older, their meals become more appetizing as parents deliver them whole fish. Young leave the nest about a month after hatching and can catch their own fish one week later.

MIGRATIONS AND MOVEMENTS

Adults remain in the Pacific Northwest year-round in areas where ice-free water is always available, such as coastal waters, large rivers, and low-elevation lakes and ponds. The nesting season begins in early to late spring, depending on the elevation of the nesting grounds. After fledglings become independent in the spring or summer, the family members disperse to defend their own foraging territories.

Female Belted Kingfisher

WHERE TO FIND BELTED KINGFISHERS

Belted Kingfishers are common residents on rivers, lakes, ponds, and bays across the Pacific Northwest. No need to plan a special trip; just visit your closest body of water to see them in action. It seems you could set up a wading pool in the back yard, stock it with goldfish, and attract a Belted Kingfisher the same day. They really are everywhere. Scan for them on exposed perches such as transmission lines and tree branches near the water, where they will be looking for their next meal. Listen for their distinctive rattling call that carries great distances across the water.

OTHER BIRDS TO SEE

If you visit a coastal bay, you might also see WESTERN GREBES, BALD EAGLES, SURF SCOTERS, BLACK TURNSTONES, Pelagic Cormorants, and COMMON LOONS.

AMERICAN DIPPER

Cinclus mexicanus

DON'T BE ALARMED if you see a songbird suddenly jump in a river and disappear. Birders know that this behavior is perfectly normal for the American Dipper, the only North American songbird that swims under water. These plucky birds enthusiastically dive into frigid water to find food, even when the air is below freezing and much of the river is iced over. Their habit of singing in the winter adds to their cheery persona.

American Dippers are solid velvety gray, with white eyelids. These sturdy little birds have short tails that they hold up at a perky angle. They are named for their habit of bobbing up and down, or dipping, while standing on a rock. Because you see them only near rushing streams, they aren't easy to mistake for any other bird.

FOOD AND FORAGING

The only songbird restricted to aquatic foraging, American Dippers take advantage of all the opportunities a swift stream provides. They find fish and aquatic invertebrates by walking along stream bottoms, picking through streamside vegetation, and haphazardly plunging themselves into the water from a standing, flying, or swimming position. They swallow small prey immediately upon capture but must process larger items, such as fish, by shaking them in their bill or slamming them against rocks. Aquatic insects make up the bulk of the bird's diet, but in some places fish are frequently captured along with tadpoles and fish eggs.

PAIRING AND PARENTING

Bulky, domed nests are built on stream banks or the undersides of bridges near clear, fast-flowing water. Each toaster-sized nest is composed of living moss, with an entrance that faces the stream. Four or five eggs are incubated for 14 to 17 days. Both parents feed young in the nest for about 25 days. Young can swim and fly short distances upon leaving the nest, but they remain in the nest area for several days. Some pairs will successfully raise a second brood of young after the first, thanks to the rapid development of nestlings and the abundant resources provided by streams.

MIGRATIONS AND MOVEMENTS

You'll find American Dippers throughout the year in areas where streams do not freeze over in the winter. Pairs begin nesting as early as February along low-elevation streams. Birds that live at higher elevations begin nesting later and must make short migrations downhill if their hunting areas become covered in ice during winter.

WHERE TO FIND AMERICAN DIPPERS

This species feasts on aquatic animals that are found only in rushing rocky streams. Look for them in the Pacific Northwest anywhere you find this type of habitat. Popular salmon- or trout-fishing streams are always a good bet. If you don't immediately see an American Dipper working the riffles, listen for the loud "jik" call that carries over the sound of the water. They often perch on favorite rocks or logs; look for traces of whitewash (bird droppings) that they leave behind.

In Washington

Mount Rainier National Park

Olympic National Park

Skagit River near Corkindale

Leavenworth National Fish Hatchery near
Leavenworth

In Oregon

Metolius River trails near Camp Sherman

Eagle Creek Fish Hatchery near Bonneville
Dam on the Columbia River

Multnomah Falls near Troutdale

Lithia Park in Ashland

Tillamook Forest Center on Highway 6

OTHER BIRDS TO SEE

Mountain streams and the forests that surround them can be full of birds, especially during breeding season. If you can tear yourself
away from the American Dippers, look for
Common Mergansers, Yellow Warblers, WEST-
ERN TANAGERS, PACIFIC WRENS, Steller's Jays,
and RED-BREASTED NUTHATCHES.

Killer Birds
BIRDS OF PREY AND OTHER MEAT-EATERS

PREDATORS ARE INHERENTLY fascinating to us, perhaps because there was a time in human history when we had to worry about being eaten ourselves. You might not get to satisfy your interest in predators by traveling to Africa and watching a cheetah take down a gazelle, but you can go to the nearest national wildlife refuge and see a Northern Harrier dive down and devour a vole. Once you adjust for scale, the spectacle is just as thrilling.

Meat-eating is such an effective survival strategy that a large and diverse group of birds are members of the carnivore club. This chapter includes the diurnal hawks, falcons, and kites; some owls; and even a killer songbird! Without these birds, we'd be awash in mice, rats, voles, and ground squirrels. Luckily, the Northwest is home to birds of prey that work night and day, in summer and winter, to catch and consume these furry morsels.

Great Horned Owl

WHITE-TAILED KITE

Elanus leucurus

WHITE-TAILED KITES float like specters over grassy fields. These pale raptors hover gracefully in the air before dropping to claim their next victim. Dramatic eye makeup gives them a moody appearance, contradicted by their habit of gathering in large groups to roost at night. They become more elusive during the nesting season, seeming to vanish from the landscape, leaving raptor lovers wanting more.

These relatively small and slight raptors have long wings and a long tail. They are eye-catching with a contrasting black, white, and gray pattern. Bold, black shoulders stand out from its light gray plumage above and below, and its namesake tail has flashy white edges. The black shading around the bird's eyes draws attention to their surprising and somewhat spooky red color. Male Northern Harriers are also gray but lack the black shoulders and clean white belly of a White-tailed Kite. Northern Harriers also have a white rump at the base of their tail.

FOOD AND FORAGING

While scanning the ground in search of prey, White-tailed Kites hover overhead by facing into the wind and rapidly beating their wings. They drop to the ground when they spot a creature to capture, grasp it in their talons, and fly it to a perch for consumption. While eating, the birds pause to scan the area for larger raptors that might attempt to steal the meal. Although they capture a variety of small animals, rodents make up the bulk of their diet.

PAIRING AND PARENTING

Pairs work together to build a nest by gathering small branches and carrying them to a tree. When all the twigs are in place, they line the nest with fine material and the female lays an average of four eggs. She incubates for at least 30 days while the male hunts and brings her food. The female stays in the nest after the young hatch and feeds them meat delivered by the male. Young are capable of flight in four to five weeks, but they require hunting instruction from their parents.

MIGRATIONS AND MOVEMENTS

In the Pacific Northwest, you'll see greater numbers of White-tailed Kites in the winter than in the spring and summer, suggesting that some migrate here from nesting grounds in other states. Pairs begin nesting in early spring, and the season can extend into the fall. Wintering birds arrive in the Northwest and begin forming large communal roosts in September; they disperse to nesting grounds by the end of May.

WHERE TO FIND WHITE-TAILED KITES

The White-tailed Kite is primarily a southern species that we are fortunate to have in the Northwest as well. Here the species is limited to southwestern Washington and western Oregon. Although some are present in the region throughout the year, they are much

more difficult to find during the nesting season. This bright bird is quite visible while perching in small trees or hovering over wetlands, grasslands, or farmed fields in search of prey. They prefer to hunt in fields where grass is allowed to grow tall enough to attract rodents. When you find such a field, watch for a flapping flash of white; the bird's hovering behavior will catch your eye.

In Washington

Nisqually National Wildlife Refuge near Olympia

Julia Butler Hansen Refuge near Cathlamet

In Oregon

Farm fields near the Nehalem Bay Sewage Ponds

Fields around the Medford Airport

William L. Finley National Wildlife Refuge near Corvallis

Fern Ridge Wildlife Management Area near Eugene

OTHER BIRDS TO SEE

A winter day spent walking along roadsides and fields may yield views of BALD EAGLES, RED-TAILED HAWKS, and COMMON RAVENS soaring above, while NORTHERN SHRIKES, Fox Sparrows, TOWNSEND'S WARBLERS, and Ruby-crowned Kinglets perch in shrubs.

NORTHERN HARRIER

Circus cyaneus

Juvenile Northern Harrier

NO OTHER BIRD of prey in the United States shows such dissimilar plumage on males and females as this open-country attention-getter. If you didn't know better, you might think the two sexes were completely different species. Northern Harriers live life in the spotlight with high-flying courtship and nesting behaviors. You might even get to look a male Harrier right in his bright yellow eyes as he cruises by just a few feet off the ground.

Plumage varies by sex and age, but all have a conspicuous white rump and bright yellow legs. Males are light gray on top, and females and juveniles are brown. Females have a streaked breast, and young birds' feathers are washed in a warm, pumpkin color. Harriers' long tails and low-flying habits make them easy to tell apart from Red-tails and other hawks.

FOOD AND FORAGING

Like owls, Northern Harriers have feathered facial discs that funnel sound to their hidden ear openings; this shape helps them hear the tiny sounds of rodents in the grass. They usually fly close to the ground, tipping side to side with wings held in a shallow V. Their broad diet includes rodents, small birds, and an occasional reptile, amphibian, or fish. In true raptor fashion, they pounce on prey with their sharp talons. Males and females differ not only in appearance but in their hunting behaviors as well, with males preferring less-vegetated sites and smaller prey than females.

PAIRING AND PARENTING

Males arrive at a nesting site first and greet the arrival of females with sky dances—U-shaped maneuvers hundreds of yards wide and 100 feet off the ground, repeated dozens of times. The male also impresses the female with an aerial transfer of prey; he flies into the air with a captured animal and drops it down to the

Male
Northern
Harrier

female flying below. After a successful court-ship, the pair builds a ground nest in a treeless area where grass or other plants are tall enough to conceal their nesting activities. The female incubates four eggs for about 30 days. The male brings her food and guards the nest when she is away searching for additional nest material and performing exercise flights. When the eggs hatch, the male performs all hunting duties for the family for the first two weeks of the nestling period. When prey is abundant, polygamous males can provide enough food to support multiple families. Nestlings can walk around the nest area at two weeks old and are capable of flight about 30 days after hatching.

MIGRATIONS AND MOVEMENTS

This species is a migrant in its northern range but it inhabits much of Oregon and Washington year-round. In coastal areas and western valleys, Northern Harriers are most common in spring, fall, and winter. During the spring and summer breeding season, they are most abundant in grasslands and wetlands east of the Cascades.

WHERE TO FIND NORTHERN HARRIERS

Just about every national wildlife refuge in Oregon and Washington offers the open, marshy habitat that attracts Northern Harriers. These generalists will show up wherever they have enough space to spread their wings without hitting a tree. Dikes and earthen berms around farmland attract burrowing rodents and the Northern Harriers that feast upon them.

They perch low, often on the ground, but they can also be found on logs and fence posts. Watch for their teetering flights low over a field. If you stare up at the sky, you'll probably miss them.

OTHER BIRDS TO SEE

At wildlife refuges in winter, it is open season on rodents for all kinds of birds and even for other mammals. Enjoying the feast could be GREAT BLUE HERONS, American Kestrels, RED-TAILED HAWKS, Rough-legged Hawks, SHORT-EARED OWLS (if you're lucky), or even a pouncing coyote.

GREAT HORNED OWL

Bubo virginianus

OCCURRING JUST ABOUT everywhere, the Great Horned is what most people think of when they hear the word "owl." Although no wiser than most birds, and less intelligent than some, the Great Horned Owl compensates with keen senses, sharp talons, and raw ferocity. They have been known to dish out cuts and concussions to anyone foolish enough to venture near their nests and will hunt anything remotely small enough to kill, including skunks and other owls.

Patterns of streaks and bars of mottled brown make the Great Horned blend in perfectly with tree bark during the day, which helps it avoid being hassled by crows. Its wide, flat face and forward-facing yellow eyes give it the human look that makes us assume advanced intelligence despite its tiny brain. The trademark points on its head are neither horns nor ears but tufts of feathers. The Northwest's only other tufted owls are the Western Screech Owl, which is much smaller and usually gray in color, and the Long-eared Owl, which is also smaller and lacks the white throat found on the Great Horned.

FOOD AND FORAGING

Great Horned Owls are flexible in the time they hunt and the animals they kill. They do most of their hunting at night, but they are active at dawn and dusk as well. Like other owls, they use their exceptional hearing and vision to locate prey. Most hunt from a perch, flying silently to the ground to pounce on a hapless animal. They swallow small prey whole but use their talons and bills to tear apart larger creatures. Prey can be as small as a grasshopper and as large as a porcupine or a Great Blue Heron.

PAIRING AND PARENTING

Like most owls, Great Horned Owls do not build their own nests. Instead, they lay their eggs in stick nests that were constructed by other species, such as Red-tailed Hawks and Common Ravens. They will also nest on the broken tops of snags, on cliffs, and on human-made structures. The female incubates two to five eggs for about 30 days, keeping the eggs warm in temperatures as low as −25 degrees Fahrenheit. When the eggs hatch, the male brings food, which the female tears apart and feeds to the nestlings. The young leave the nest six weeks after hatching but can barely fly, if at all, and spend their time perched in nearby branches or on the ground.

MIGRATIONS AND MOVEMENTS

These hardy souls can, in most cases, withstand extremely cold temperatures and adjust their behavior to consume whatever animals are available. Pairs can therefore remain in a breeding territory year-round. Rearing young requires a big time commitment. Females lay their eggs in the winter, and pairs feed nestlings in the spring and continue to care for fledglings throughout the summer.

WHERE TO FIND GREAT HORNED OWLS

Great Horned Owls occupy a variety of natural areas and are also at home in cities and farms, as long as perches and nest sites are available. They are easiest to spot when on a nest, especially in winter, when many trees are leafless. The owl's tufted head is a dead giveaway,

poking out of an old stick nest. Look for them hunting at dawn and dusk, when you might see them in flight or perched above their hunting grounds. Their call, a stereotypical series of deep hoots, is a great indication that you are in the right place.

In Washington

Ridgefield National Wildlife Refuge near
  Vancouver

Nisqually National Wildlife Refuge near
  Olympia

Cowiche Canyon near Yakima

Skagit Wildlife Area near Mount Vernon

In Oregon

Sauvie Island near Portland

Tryon Creek State Park in Portland

Fernhill Wetlands near Forest Grove

William L. Finley National Wildlife Refuge
  near Corvallis

OTHER BIRDS TO SEE

Crepuscular animals, active at dawn and dusk, take advantage of a time when many prey animals begin to emerge from their daytime hiding places. American Robins and SWAINSON'S THRUSHES sing the last songs of the day as the sun goes down, COMMON NIGHTHAWKS and a variety of bats take flight to enjoy the feast of insects, and Western Screech Owls and Barred Owls prepare for their nocturnal excursions.

SHORT-EARED OWL

Asio flammeus

FLITTING AND DIVING as if controlled by invisible marionette strings, Short-eared Owls mesmerize with their intricate flight. Like a feathered, predatory butterfly, they zigzag low across fields in search of small mammals. This owl, never a pillar of reliability, will up and leave if it finds better hunting elsewhere. On the bright side, Short-eared Owls are easy to locate if you visit the right place, because they prefer open country and hunt during the day.

The owl's plumage is a mosaic of buff-colored and brown tones that allow it to disappear in a field of dry brown grass. Its chest is boldly streaked, and its wings are crisscrossed with spots and stripes. Dark crescents on its wrists stand out when it flies. Its face seems a little too small for its body, and it has a blunt look in flight, as if it flew face-first into the side of a barn.

FOOD AND FORAGING

The Short-eared Owl flies silently several feet above the ground, tilting itself back and forth and listening for prey. When it locates an animal, it drops suddenly to the ground and captures it with its talons. Short-eareds hunt primarily small mammals and birds, with rodent populations dictating where they nest and spend the winter.

PAIRING AND PARENTING

In the spring, males perform a spectacular courtship flight that involves an upward spiral, a song, a stooping dive, and a series of loud wing claps. If the female approves, she joins him in the flight, and they remain paired for the nesting season. Short-eareds are unique among owls in that they construct their own nest by scraping a depression in the ground and lining it with grass and feathers. The number of eggs laid is variable, ranging from one to eleven. After the eggs hatch in 25 to 30 days, the male captures prey and the female feeds it to the nestlings. Nestlings leave the nest 14 to 17 days after hatching, but they are unable to fly. They wander off in various directions, perhaps to dilute predation risk, and receive care from their parents for several more weeks.

MIGRATIONS AND MOVEMENTS

Short-eared Owls begin nesting from March to May, and young become independent by the end of summer. At the end of the nesting season, individuals migrate to wherever prey densities are high. Large concentrations winter in northwest Washington, arriving in September and departing for their nesting grounds in the spring.

WHERE TO FIND SHORT-EARED OWLS

During the winter, they seem to be more concentrated in northwest Washington than anywhere else in the region. Watch for them in open country, which they favor for hunting. They breed primarily on the east side of the Cascades but are more difficult to find there because they are present in much lower densities. Finding a Short-eared Owl perched on or near the ground, where they like to be, can be next to impossible. Tripping on one is about as likely as seeing it before it flushes into the air. Watch for them flapping acrobatically over the fields; their long wings, buff color, and stiff wing beats make them instantly identifiable.

In Washington

Samish Flats near Burlington

Skagit Wildlife Area near Mount Vernon

Fort Flagler State Park near Port Townsend

Nisqually National Wildlife Refuge near Olympia

In Oregon

William L. Finley National Wildlife Refuge near Corvallis

Fern Ridge Wildlife Management Area near Eugene

Fields surrounding Medford Airport

OTHER BIRDS TO SEE

Places with lots of Short-eared Owls in the winter are also likely to attract other raptors such as BALD EAGLES, Rough-legged Hawks, NORTHERN HARRIERS, Merlins, PEREGRINE FALCONS, and (sometimes) Snowy Owls.

PRAIRIE FALCON

Falco mexicanus

PRAIRIE FALCONS SURVEY their realm from the castlelike rock outcroppings on which they nest. Hard-working ground squirrels toil below, unaware until it's too late that one of their number has been dispatched by this skilled hunter of the open country.

Prairie Falcons are the faded brown color of many dry-country birds. Their dark backs and pale undersides create counter-shading that hides them against the sky from below and against the ground from above. Their faces are distinctive, with a white eyebrow stripe and brown mustache stripe. Dark patches on both sides of its body under the wings distinguish it from other falcons, and its pointed wings and rapid wing beats in the air distinguish it from hawks.

FOOD AND FORAGING

The most common prey items captured by Prairie Falcons are ground squirrels and Horned Larks. They often fly several feet above the ground and then close in on their prey while gliding at an even lower altitude, grabbing their quarry in their talons and carrying it to a perch to consume it.

PAIRING AND PARENTING

Pairs begin nesting in early spring to ensure that the hatching of their young coincides with the emergence of juvenile ground squirrels. They nest on cliffs, rock outcroppings, and human-made structures. Adults do not construct the nest, however; instead, the female scrapes a depression in debris or lays her four to five eggs in an old nest of another species.

After the nestlings hatch in 30 to 40 days, they are fed ground squirrels that were captured by the male and torn to pieces by the female. After four weeks, parents leave prey items at the edge of the nest for the young to eat on their own. The young leave the nest 38 days after hatching, but their parents feed them for another month.

MIGRATIONS AND MOVEMENTS

Adults arrive at their nesting sites by the end of March and depart in July after nesting is complete and the ground squirrels have moved underground to escape the high temperatures. At this time, Prairie Falcons move to mountainous areas, where small mammals remain active at the higher elevations. As winter approaches, they leave high-elevation areas and continue to wander, with some individuals visiting the westside valleys of Oregon and Washington, including the Willamette Valley, the Rogue River Valley, and the Puget Trough.

WHERE TO FIND PRAIRIE FALCONS

The best place to find a Prairie Falcon depends on the time of year. In the spring and early summer, look on the dry side (the east side) of the Cascades in places with rocky cliffs for nesting. In the fall, look for them at higher elevations in the Cascades. During the winter, you'll see them almost anywhere in the Northwest, but in low numbers. Look for a brown bird perched on a utility pole in open country or flapping its way back to its rocky nest.

In Washington

Samish Flats near Burlington (winter)

Flying above open areas of the Sunrise Visitor Center in Mount Rainier National Park (fall)

Toppenish National Wildlife Refuge near Yakima (nesting)

The cliffs of Yakima Canyon from State Route 821 (nesting)

In Oregon

Around Timberline Lodge on Mount Hood (fall)

Fort Rock State Park near La Pine (nesting)

Lower Klamath National Wildlife Refuge near Klamath Falls (winter)

Smith Rock State Park near Redmond (nesting)

OTHER BIRDS TO SEE

Rocky outcroppings in the dry, open country are magnets for nesting birds. Prairie Falcons share these high-rises with COMMON RAVENS, GOLDEN EAGLES, Barn Owls, White-throated Swifts, Cliff Swallows, and CANYON WRENS.

NORTHERN SHRIKE

Lanius excubitor

IF STRENGTH WERE measured by the size of prey an animal kills relative to its own size, the Northern Shrike would be among the world's toughest birds. This songbird can kill birds and mammals nearly twice its own weight and then carry them in flight to a perch, where a macabre butchering process occurs. With its black mask, the Northern Shrike resembles a superhero, but it behaves like a villain, given its habit of impaling prey on thorns and barbed wire.

Northern Shrikes look quite similar to their sister species, the Loggerhead Shrike, which is not found west of the Cascades. Both species have gray heads and backs with black wings, tails, and masks. Their chests are white, as is a patch on each wing. The differences between the two are subtle. Loggerheads' black masks go all the way across their foreheads over their beaks, but Northerns have gray foreheads. Northerns also have a longer, more hooked bill.

FOOD AND FORAGING

Most of the creatures captured by Northern Shrikes are insects, but birds and mammals make up a majority of the biomass that this bird consumes. These predators hunt by scanning for prey from a perch and then pouncing on their meal on the ground, in a shrub, or in a tree. Shrikes capture small prey, such as insects and shrews, with their bills, but they use their feet to grab larger prey, such as birds and voles. They are called butcherbirds because they impale their prey on thorns or barbed wire fences. Then they remove and discard inedible pieces and select edible portions to swallow. They also use impaling as a means to store prey during periods of productive hunting.

PAIRING AND PARENTING

Both adults build the nest, a bulky cup, in conifers, deciduous trees, or shrubs. The female incubates the four to nine eggs for 17 days. Early in the nestling period, the male captures prey and delivers it to the female so she can break off bite-sized pieces for the young, who leave the nest about 20 days after hatching. Twenty days after they leave the nest, young are capable of catching and impaling their own insects.

MIGRATIONS AND MOVEMENTS

Northern Shrikes begin nesting in early spring and depart their boreal nesting grounds at the end of summer, arriving in the Pacific Northwest by the end of October. Most of these winter visitors depart the region in February or March.

WHERE TO FIND NORTHERN SHRIKES

Wintering birds choose hunting grounds where open areas with good visibility are adjacent to scattered trees and shrubs for perching. Farm country and wildlife refuges are great places to look for them. They tend to choose conspicuous perches in shrubs and on posts. Because its light gray color is unique for a Northwest bird of its size, a shrike is easy to spot while you are traveling by car.

In Washington

Skagit Wildlife Area near Mount Vernon

Marymoor Park in Redmond

Toppenish National Wildlife Refuge near
 Yakima

Nisqually National Wildlife Refuge near
 Olympia

In Oregon

Jackson Bottom Wetlands Preserve near
 Hillsboro

William L. Finley National Wildlife Refuge
 near Corvallis

Fields surrounding the Medford Airport

Fern Ridge Wildlife Management Area near
 Eugene

OTHER BIRDS TO SEE

Hedgerows and fields are full of songbirds during the winter, but only one of them is trying to eat the others. Hiding in the blackberry bushes to escape the notice of a Northern Shrike could be Fox Sparrows, Savannah Sparrows, Lincoln's Sparrows, White-crowned Sparrows, Golden-crowned Sparrows, Marsh Wrens, and Ruby-crowned Kinglets.

Marathon Birds
RACKING UP THE FREQUENT FLYER MILES

IMAGINE TRAVELING THOUSANDS of miles, nearly nonstop, on a diet of grass and berries. A feat like this is not only possible, but is a biyearly event for some birds, whose ordinary appearances belie their identities as migration superheroes. The great distances covered by their migrations are nearly incomprehensible.

Everyone knows that many North American birds fly south for the winter. In the Pacific Northwest, however, an ideal combination of mild winter conditions and productive marine areas attracts birds from all directions during every season of the year. Some birds arrive from nesting grounds in the extreme northern reaches of North America, using our region as a winter locale or a rest and refueling station. Some serious travelers spend their lives in constant summer, finding food near the Northwest Coast during our summer and then returning to the Southern Hemisphere during our winter. Others nest in Northern Europe and Asia but cross borders and oceans to winter among our resident birds—no passport required.

Six migratory birds are standouts whose return we anticipate each year. Our favorite marathon birds include three types of waterfowl, two ocean-going birds, and a large and whimsical shorebird. When you see these endurance athletes on the beach, in a park, or in the sea, be thankful that the Pacific Northwest is such a magnet for world travelers.

Male Eurasian Wigeon

BRANT

Branta bernicla

THESE UNASSUMING GEESE could easily slip under your radar if you are accustomed to the bombast of Snow Geese and Canada Geese. Brant are mellow vegetarians whose volume rarely rises above a subdued chatter as they feed and relax in coastal bays. One of the great things about Brant is that you rarely see just one. On their annual migration, they gather by the thousands and make quite an engaging natural spectacle as they simultaneously slurp eelgrass. They are much beloved by the communities they visit each spring as they migrate through the Salish Sea, and annual festivals are held in their honor in Washington and on the Canadian side at Vancouver Island.

The Brant is a small, dark goose with a black head, a white rump, and a white collar below its chin. These field marks distinguish the species from Canada and Cackling Geese, which have white cheeks.

FOOD AND FORAGING

No other North American goose has a diet as specialized as the Brant, which feeds on eelgrass, green algae, and salt marsh vegetation. Flocks find vegetation by walking through exposed tidal flats or by floating in bays when the tide returns. After it pulls long blades of eelgrass into its bill, like a hungry person slurping spaghetti, the Brant uses its tongue to fold each blade into a little wad before swallowing.

PAIRING AND PARENTING

Females construct a simple nest on the arctic tundra of western and northern Alaska by scraping a depression in the permafrost. The nest cup is lined with vegetation and a mass of their own downy feathers. Three to five eggs are incubated for 23 days. When the female leaves the nest on occasion to fuel up on plants, the male guards the eggs but does not incubate—the downy feathers applied by the female help keep the eggs from cooling. One day after hatching, young can leave the nest to find food, but they must be brooded by their mother to keep warm when they are not walking or eating. While the female keeps them warm, the father provides protection by chasing away potential predators. Young can fly when they are 40 days old and eventually migrate with their parents to the wintering grounds.

MIGRATIONS AND MOVEMENTS

After breeding at the extreme western and northern edges of Alaska, West Coast populations of Brant migrate as far south as Mexico. Before the big push south, however, thousands gather in September and October at staging areas on the Alaskan peninsula to fill up on eelgrass. Flocks arrive at their warm coastal wintering sites by late October or early November. In March, they begin departing for their northern nesting grounds. Brant traveling north visit the coasts of Oregon and Washington in April and May.

WHERE TO FIND BRANT

Wintering and migratory flocks occupy coastal areas of Oregon and Washington. Look for a group of dark birds resting on a sandbar or swimming in the calm waters of a bay. While walking along a beach, you might see a flock of Brant cruising above the surf.

In Washington

Dungeness National Wildlife Refuge near Sequim

Willapa Bay near Long Beach

Padilla Bay near Burlington

Samish Bay near Burlington

Discovery Park, West Point, in Seattle

In Oregon

Yaquina Bay in Newport

Bayocean Spit on Tillamook Bay near Tillamook

Netarts Bay near Netarts

OTHER BIRDS TO SEE

Dungeness Bay is a popular wintering location for Brant and a great place to see the abundant seabirds that seek shelter there from winter waves. Look for SURF SCOTERS, WESTERN GREBES, HARLEQUIN DUCKS, RED-BREASTED MERGANSERS, COMMON LOONS, Pacific Loons, and Red-throated Loons. If you are lucky, you'll see a Yellow-billed Loon.

CACKLING GOOSE
Branta hutchinsii

FOR THOSE WHO are intimidated by the large, pushy Canada Geese that gather in parks and golf courses, Cackling Geese are a smaller, cuter version with a better work ethic. These mini-geese are barely larger than a duck, and their short beaks and squarish heads give them the look of a plush toy. Don't get between them and a choice bite of grass, however—they can turn feisty and hiss just like a full-sized goose. Although they are small, Cackling Geese embroider the whole sky with the interconnected Vs of their huge flocks, deafening you with their high-pitched cackling in one of the Northwest's signature sights and sounds of fall.

This species has markings similar to those of the Canada Goose, from which it was recently separated as its own species. Both have a black neck and head with white cheeks and grayish brown wings. Cacklers vary in size, but they are usually smaller with a stubbier beak and shorter neck than Canada Geese. They may also have a white collar at the base of their neck that is absent on Canadas. Their call is higher pitched than a Canada's call and sounds less like a honk and more like a yelp.

FOOD AND FORAGING

Like a herd of miniature bison, wintering flocks of Cacklers march through fields of grass, alfalfa, barley, and wheat, plucking the tips from tender shoots in their path. Their diet is a little more complex in Canada or Alaska, where they fatten up on leaves and berries throughout the summer before departing south for the winter.

PAIRING AND PARENTING

Cacklers nest on islands off the Alaskan coast or on the mainland near bodies of water. Unlike most ducks, male geese guard females during nesting and may stand guard at the nest while the female takes an incubation break. Incubation lasts 25 days. Within one day of hatching, the precocious goslings, usually five of them, follow their parents to areas of short grass and sedge, where they can safely graze and capture insects. The mother keeps the goslings warm by brooding them when necessary, and the father keeps a keen eye out for predators. Young Cacklers can fly about 40 days after hatching, at which time the family joins a flock with other families.

MIGRATIONS AND MOVEMENTS

After nesting in Canada or Alaska, thousands of Cacklers gather in late September in staging areas such as the Alaskan Peninsula to bulk up on leaves and berries. Large flocks then fly directly to western Oregon and Washington on a two- to four-day flight, arriving by mid-October. After a winter of eating grass in the rain, they depart Oregon and Washington in mid- to late April and arrive at their nesting grounds ready to nest by late May.

WHERE TO FIND CACKLING GEESE

Cacklers winter in Washington and Oregon, in large flocks that feast on grass in fields, rest on a body of water, or call to one another as they fly overhead. From October to April each year, a unique group of Cacklers gathers in a dairy pasture northeast of Pacific City, Oregon. This flock of more than 100 geese makes up the entire breeding population of the tiny Semidi Islands in Alaska. They don't seem to mix with other Cackling Geese, and they return every year to this small, wet field. Each night they fly out to the ocean to roost on nearby Haystack Rock, or to ride the waves around it. You'll know for sure that you have found a Semidi Island goose if you see the blue-green plastic collars that biologists have attached to some of them to track their survival.

In Washington

Golf courses and bays in Ocean Shores

Julia Butler Hansen Refuge near Cathlamet

Nisqually National Wildlife Refuge near Olympia

Sikes Lake near Carnation

In Oregon

Pacific City for Semidi Islands Cackling Geese

Sauvie Island near Portland

Fernhill Wetlands near Forest Grove

Ankeny National Wildlife Refuge near Albany

William L. Finley National Wildlife Refuge near Corvallis

OTHER BIRDS TO SEE

If you go to Pacific City to check out the Semidi Islands geese, visit the Nestucca Bay National Wildlife Refuge to find dark chocolate-colored Dusky Canada Geese (a darker subspecies of Canada Goose), WHITE-TAILED KITES, Merlins, BELTED KINGFISHERS, Northern Pintails, and an abundance of other waterfowl.

EURASIAN WIGEON

Anas penelope

Female (left)
and male(right)
Eurasian
Wigeons with
American
Wigeons (back-
ground)

EVERY WINTER, American Wigeons are visited by their exotic cousins from Siberia. Eurasian Wigeons seem to fit in well with the locals, joining huge wintering flocks as they graze and paddle the shallows of Northwest waterways. Their gregarious nature and boisterous squeaking make every day seem like a rowdy wigeon family reunion. In the Pacific Northwest, we are fortunate to enjoy the highest concentrations of these attractive little ducks in the Lower 48. A Eurasian Wigeon sighting is a splendid reward for birders taking the time to examine large flocks of American Wigeons in winter.

Thanks to their rusty heads and light gray backs and flanks, male Eurasians stand out in a crowd of American Wigeons. Both species have whitish foreheads, but an American lacks any red color on its head, has rufous (reddish)

flanks, and has a green stripe that stretches from the eye to the back of the head. Females are more difficult to distinguish, but Eurasian hens' heads are warmer colored than gray-headed Americans.

FOOD AND FORAGING

Wigeons are the greatest grazers of the dabbling ducks. In the Pacific Northwest, Eurasian Wigeons pluck grass and other plants from the ground alongside American Wigeons and Canada Geese in city parks and along shorelines. They will also swim for aquatic vegetation, but they spend less time dabbling with their heads under water than ducks such as Mallards. During the breeding season, Eurasians supplement their diet with aquatic insects, mollusks, and crustaceans.

PAIRING AND PARENTING

This species nests in the northern portions of Europe and Asia, from Iceland to Siberia. They begin nesting in late spring after the ice and snow melt away from their nesting grounds. Females provide care for the young, incubating eight or nine eggs in a well-camouflaged ground nest for 25 days. After the brood hatches, the female leads them to aquatic and upland sites, where they can graze on vegetation and capture aquatic insects.

MIGRATIONS AND MOVEMENTS

When the nesting season is complete, Eurasian Wigeons disperse throughout the Northern and Southern Hemispheres. In addition to Oregon and Washington, these wanderers will winter in southern Eurasia, Africa, Southeast Asia, and the Middle East. They remain in our area from October through April. Females usually return to the area where they hatched to breed each year, but males probably pair with a different female each season.

WHERE TO FIND EURASIAN WIGEONS

Eurasian Wigeons are never especially abundant, but if you find a large enough flock of American Wigeons, there's bound to be one or two Eurasians in there somewhere. Look for wigeon flocks nibbling on grass or gathered in marshes, shallow lakes, or bays. Their call sounds a lot like a dog's squeaky toy being squeezed.

In Washington

Samish Island and Samish Flats near Burlington

Padilla Bay near Burlington

Point No Point Lighthouse and County Park near Kingston

Ridgefield National Wildlife Refuge near Vancouver

In Oregon

William L. Finley National Wildlife Refuge near Corvallis

Bayocean Spit on Tillamook Bay near Tillamook

Tualatin River National Wildlife Refuge near Sherwood

Westmoreland Park in Portland

OTHER BIRDS TO SEE

When you visit Tillamook Bay during the winter, look for BRANT, WESTERN GREBES, Horned Grebes, BALD EAGLES, White-winged Scoters, and COMMON LOONS.

BLACK-FOOTED ALBATROSS

Phoebastria nigripes

ALBATROSSES ARE LEGENDARY long-distance travelers of the southern seas. They glide above the waves on wings that can span the width of a queen-size bed. Luckily, those of us bound to the Pacific Northwest have an excellent opportunity to view albatrosses that regularly visit our corner of the world. All you need is a stomach strong enough to endure a boat ride at least 20 miles out into the Pacific Ocean and back. The Black-footed Albatross has been described as a "feathered pig" because of its enthusiasm for scraps of food tossed overboard, and offering them food in this way is often the best way to see them. Despite such an unflattering description, this bird deserves admiration for the thousands of miles each individual flies in search of food—both natural and human-supplied.

With its long, narrow wings and oceanic habits, this species looks like no other bird—except another albatross. Black-footeds are generally darker in color than their kin and have heavy bills with hooked tips. Laysan Albatrosses, also found far off the coast of the Pacific Northwest, are a similar size but have white heads and lighter plumage overall.

FOOD AND FORAGING

Albatrosses are in the minority of birds that possess a sense of smell. For this reason, they are attracted to fishing boats discarding bits of their catch. When not following boats, Black-footeds pursue food they find at the ocean surface, including flying squid, flying fish, and the eggs of flying fish, which are often attached to floating objects. They capture their food while floating on the ocean like giant ducks, lazily dipping their heads into the water or diving a few feet below the surface.

PAIRING AND PARENTING

Black-footed Albatrosses nest on the ground in large colonies on Pacific Islands near Hawaii, Japan, and China. Reproduction is a slow process, with birds waiting until they are at least five years old to breed, laying only one egg per year, and skipping nesting during years when conditions are not quite right. The parents take turns incubating the egg in nonstop shifts that can exceed 30 days. Adults take turns brooding and guarding the nestling for its first 20 days. By the time it is 30 days old, the nestling is unguarded and must wait 2 to 10 days for its parent to return with a meal. After about five months, the chick finally leaves the nest and gathers with other fledglings on a beach before they all take their first flight.

MIGRATIONS AND MOVEMENTS

The marathon nesting season of the Black-footed Albatross begins when adults return to island nesting colonies in November or December and ends when fledglings take to the sea in the summer. After nesting, adults wander the northeastern Pacific, spending their time flying above the waves, capturing food near the sea surface, or resting on the water. They are most frequently seen near our coasts from April through late October, but you can find immature birds throughout the year.

WHERE TO FIND BLACK-FOOTED ALBATROSSES

Albatrosses are rarely seen from land. The best way to get a good look is to take a daylong boat trip into the ocean (a pelagic trip) to the places many miles offshore where albatrosses feed. These trips run regularly spring through fall out of Westport, Washington, and Newport, Oregon. Albatrosses are much larger and have much longer wings than other pelagic birds, which makes identifying them easy. You might see one soaring low over the waves or feeding while floating on the ocean.

OTHER BIRDS TO SEE

Pelagic trips are an amazing opportunity to find birds that you will never see from land and to get better looks at those of which you've had only unsatisfying glimpses. Depending on the time of year, you could see SOOTY SHEARWATERS, Northern Fulmars, MARBLED MURRELETS, PIGEON GUILLEMOTS, Fork-tailed Storm Petrels, and Pomarine Jaegers.

SOOTY SHEARWATER

Puffinus griseus

SOOTY SHEARWATERS MIGHT be the most gregarious seabirds in the world. Feeding in flocks of thousands and nesting in colonies of millions, these birds obviously have little regard for personal space. Huge flocks of them grace our coastal waters from spring to fall, returning to their breeding sites in the South Pacific to nest when it is our winter and their summer—an ideal lifestyle for anyone wanting to travel the globe and avoid winter weather!

Shearwaters are named for their long, bladelike wings that seem to slice through the air above the waves. Their wings are attached about halfway down their bodies, making them look different from gulls, whose wings start just behind their heads. Sooties hold their wings out straight as they glide between rapid, shallow wing beats. They have long, skinny bills with a hooked tip and tube-shaped nostrils on the top that are used for smelling food and excreting oceanic salts. Their dark gray plumage and silvery underwings distinguish them from the less common Short-tailed Shearwater, a similar species with darker underwings.

FOOD AND FORAGING

Sooties can dive to depths of more than 200 feet, propelling themselves by beating their wings. While diving, they capture a variety of marine animals such as shrimp, squid, and fish. Feeding flocks in the hundreds of thousands gather off Pacific Northwest shores to pursue schools of anchovies. They will also pick up discards from fishing boats from the water's surface, making them easy to spot on pelagic birding expeditions.

PAIRING AND PARENTING

Sooties nest when it is summer in the South Pacific and winter in the North, in colonies of up to 2.7 million pairs on islands near Australia, New Zealand, and Chile. Adults dig nest burrows in islands with soft soils or place their nests in crevices on rocky islands. The single egg is incubated or 55 days by both parents, who feed the youngster by regurgitating food obtained in deep sea dives, some of which occur in Antarctic waters at least 900 miles from their nest site. Because of their parents' long foraging flights, chicks must wait up to 15 days between meals during the 80 to 100 days that they spend in the burrow.

MIGRATIONS AND MOVEMENTS

After nesting in the Southern Hemisphere, Sooties flee the southern winter for the northern summer. This requires an extraordinary migration to one of three oceanic "wintering" areas: the waters off the West Coast of the United States, the western Pacific off the coasts of Japan and Russia, or the Bering Sea and Gulf of Alaska. The voyage from south to north and back can exceed 40,000 miles. In a single year, some individuals fly over the entire expanse of the Pacific Ocean from just north of Antarctica to the Bering Sea. They are found off the Northwest Coast from March to November.

WHERE TO FIND SOOTY SHEARWATERS

You rarely find a Sooty flying over the beach, so you'll need to set your sights offshore. Shearwaters fly low over the ocean, surfing the air currents produced by the waves. During fall migration in August and September, you might see a string of them fly by if you watch the ocean with binoculars or a spotting scope. In fall, they often join feeding flocks of gulls near the mouths of bays and rivers; these flocks can sometimes comprise hundreds or thousands of birds.

In Washington

Tokeland, at the mouth of Willapa Bay

Ferry from Port Angeles to Victoria, British
Columbia (in the air and on the water)

Cape Flattery near Neah Bay

Columbia River, North Jetty, near Ilwaco

In Oregon

Columbia River, South Jetty, in Fort Stevens
State Park near Astoria

Boiler Bay State Scenic Viewpoint near Depoe
Bay

Pelagic boat trip out of Newport

Barview Jetty at the mouth of Tillamook Bay

OTHER BIRDS TO SEE

The places where fresh water rushes out to
mix with salt water at the mouth of bays and
rivers are rich with nutrients and full of fish.
Sooty Shearwaters might be mingling there
with CASPIAN TERNS, BROWN PELICANS,
BRANDT'S CORMORANTS, SURF SCOTERS, and
plenty of gulls.

WHIMBREL

Numenius phaeopus

ON A FOGGY coastal morning, the unmistakable silhouette of a Whimbrel materializes in the distance. It walks carefully across the sand with its companions, stopping to pluck a small creature out of a hole with its long, curved bill and gobble it down. As you approach, it takes to the air on long, pointed wings and glides to a safer location. Most Whimbrels that we see in the Pacific Northwest are bound for nesting grounds to the north or wintering grounds to the south, but a precious few stick around throughout the summer. Make the most of every Whimbrel sighting, because you never know when the next will occur.

Whimbrels are large, comical shorebirds. Picture a pigeon with tall legs and a long, drooping bill. Its head is marked with alternating light and dark stripes that extend from its bill to the back of its head. It is easily distinguished from the closely related Long-billed Curlew, which has an outrageously long bill and an unstriped head.

FOOD AND FORAGING

The Whimbrel's bill is perfectly suited to reaching intertidal invertebrates hiding in their burrows. This unique bill actually matches the curvature of crab burrows in some areas.

Like other shorebirds, Whimbrels capture a variety of invertebrate prey on coastal winter grounds and migration stopover sites. Upon reaching nesting sites in Alaska and Canada, the Whimbrel switches to a diet of terrestrial insects and berries.

PAIRING AND PARENTING

As soon as the snow clears from their tundra nesting sites, males advertise their territory by flying several hundred feet into air and descending to the ground while singing, gliding, and spiraling. Both parents incubate the clutch of four eggs for about 25 days and care for the young, which leave their shallow ground nest a few hours after hatching. Eventually, the male is left to care for the chicks until he migrates south. The youngsters will head south on their own a month later.

MIGRATIONS AND MOVEMENTS

In the summer and fall, North American Whimbrels migrate from northern nesting grounds to their incredibly expansive wintering grounds—an area that stretches from the West Coast of North America to the southern tip of South America. During these trips, they make several nonstop flights over the open ocean before resting and refueling on coastal beaches. These rest stops provide excellent opportunities for northwestern birders to view this intrepid species. During their southbound migration, Whimbrels refuel on the Northwest Coast from July through October. Northbound migrants return to the region from March to May, while a few nonbreeders spend the entire summer on the coast.

WHERE TO FIND WHIMBRELS

Whimbrels are most abundant in the Northwest during their spring and fall migrations. You'll see them probing for food on beaches, mudflats, and wet fields. They are much taller than all those stubby sandpipers and are easily visible as they stroll along beaches and through grassy fields, although their brown color offers them a little camouflage.

In Washington

Oyhut Wildlife Recreation Area in Ocean Shores

Crockett Lake on Whidbey Island

Butler Flats near Burlington

Ediz Hook near Port Angeles

In Oregon

Bayocean Spit in Tillamook Bay near Tillamook

Siltcoos River Estuary near Florence

Yaquina Bay in Newport

Siletz Bay near Taft

OTHER BIRDS TO SEE

During spring migration on the coast, Whimbrels are joined by Black-bellied Plovers, GREAT BLUE HERONS, and a collection of sandpipers so abundant and diverse that you'll be either fascinated or frustrated with identifying them all.

Singing Birds
MEMORABLE CALLS
AND SONGS

THE PLEASANT CACOPHONY of birdsong provides the soundtrack
to our springs and summers. Whether a sweet melody or a unique
call, these songs wake us up at first light and sing us through to
sunset. Birdsongs also create a sense of place for us. What would
a canyon be without the wren named for it, or a summer camping
trip without the ethereal song of the Swainson's Thrush at dusk?
These amazing vocalizations aren't made for us, but we enjoy them
just the same. The birds (most often males) are attracting mates
or staking a claim to a territory. If we translated their songs, they
might be romantic ballads for the ladies or a strongly worded
tongue lashing for a rival male.

Two of the species included here are not technically classified
as songbirds, but their vocalizations are so distinct that you will
instantly recognize them after you have learned their sounds. The
others are true songbirds, a diverse grouping with more than 4000
species worldwide. These birds use a series of tiny membranes
embedded in their airways to produce songs, some of which are so
complex that the human voice box can only poorly imitate them.

Pacific Wren

CALIFORNIA QUAIL

Callipepla californica

WHAT COULD BE cuter than a California Quail that sports sharp colors, a beach ball body, and bobbing plumes on its head? It scurries through the brush willy-nilly when disturbed, and in the summer it's followed by a herd of fluffy youngsters. Males would probably prefer to be described as handsome, as they perch proudly out in the open to display their eye-catching plumage. Not musical at all, a California Quail's calls sound more like speech. They rally one another with their unmistakable "Chi-CA-go!" call, and males advertise their territories with a repeated "Wah!"

California Quail are instantly recognizable by their pot-bellied silhouette with the distinctive topknot. Males have intricate plumage, including a black face that is outlined in white. Females are browner and lack the bright pattern on the face. Mountain Quail, the other Northwest quail, have a topknot that is straight like an exclamation point; a California's topknot looks more like a question mark drooping forward over its face.

Male California Quail

FOOD AND FORAGING

California Quail pick at seeds and other plant parts found in gaps between brushy areas. During summer, much of their diet comprises soft plants such as clover and lupine. During the rest of the year, they eat berries and buds of woody plants as well as grass seed and a few insects.

PAIRING AND PARENTING

When nesting time arrives, females build a simple nest of grass and weeds on the ground in an area well hidden by vegetation. She can lay more than 20 eggs and usually performs all of the incubation duties during the 23-day period, although her mate may chip in or guard the nest. The chicks leave the nest immediately after hatching. For the next two to three months, the parents brood the chicks to keep them warm, lead them to food, and protect them from predators. Occasionally, communal families form, with several adults watching out for chicks from multiple nests. When the young can fly at three months, they join coveys (groups of 30 to 70 individuals) with their parents.

MIGRATIONS AND MOVEMENTS

California Quail are permanent residents of Oregon and Washington. Coveys form at the end of the summer nesting season and wander within a home range but rarely move more than 10 miles from one location to another during the year. They dissolve in the spring when birds start pairing off in anticipation of nesting.

WHERE TO FIND CALIFORNIA QUAIL

Once found only in California and the southwestern corner of Oregon, thousands of California Quail were captured and released throughout Oregon and Washington in the nineteenth and twentieth centuries to increase bird-hunting opportunities. They are now common in valleys and low areas on the east side of the Cascades, but you can find them on the west side as well. They need some hiding places, so they prefer areas with thick brush instead of farm fields that offer only low vegetation. They often run along roads and perch on fence posts. You can hear their distinctive three-note call from a great distance.

In Washington

Wenas Basin between Yakima and Ellensburg

Dungeness National Wildlife Refuge near Sequim

Wenatchee Confluence State Park in Wenatchee

Magnuson Park in Seattle

In Oregon

Fort Rock State Park near La Pine

Jackson Bottom Wetlands Preserve near Hillsboro

Prescott Park in Medford

Baskett Slough National Wildlife Refuge near Dallas

OTHER BIRDS TO SEE

Take a road trip through the farmland and sagebrush of the east side of the Pacific Northwest and you'll have miles and miles of fences to check for open-country birds such as MOUNTAIN and WESTERN BLUEBIRDS, WESTERN KINGBIRDS, American Kestrels, Loggerhead Shrikes, and WESTERN MEADOWLARKS.

COMMON NIGHTHAWK

Chordeiles minor

COMMON NIGHTHAWKS WAIT until the month of June to return to the Northwest and fill the sky with their unique sounds and distinctive flight. They make a characteristic, nasal-toned "meeernt" that will alert you to their presence even when they are flying high above. Nighthawks also sing with their feathers, making a booming "vrrrum" with their wings in a noisy diving courtship display.

The odd-looking Common Nighthawk spends most of the day perfectly hidden in plain sight and then emerges into a summer evening to feast on mosquitoes. Their mottled brown feathers camouflage well against a variety of backdrops, whether they are nesting or roosting. In flight, their long, pointed wings and long tail make them much more noticeable. As they hunt, their tiny beaks gape open to catch insects. A white throat and white wing bars help to distinguish this species from the rarer Common Poorwill that is darker and stubbier overall.

FOOD AND FORAGING

Despite their name, Common Nighthawks are not hawks or birds of prey. They eat small insects, which they capture with their wide mouths while flying with batlike wing beats during dusk and dawn. Short, bristled feathers that help them catch aerial insects surround their beaks. Their unfortunate predatory misnomer has resulted in persecution by humans who sought to protect their farm animals from predators. Small birds also mistake Common Nighthawks for enemies such as owls and mob them as they try to rest during the day.

PAIRING AND PARENTING

Although they are quite conspicuous while hunting insects in the sky, Common Nighthawks are masters of camouflage at their nests. The female lays a pair of eggs directly on the ground or, in some cases, on a rooftop. While incubating, she is almost invisible against the backdrop of gravel, sand, or debris surrounding the nest. When she is off the nest, her eggs are nearly invisible as well. After 18 days, nestlings hatch as camouflaged, semi-mobile puffs. They are sheltered from the hot sun by the female during the day, while the male hunts and brings the family food. The young can fly 18 days after hatching and will eventually join a migratory flock with their parents.

MIGRATIONS AND MOVEMENTS

These extreme long-distance migrants spend their winters in South America as far south as Buenos Aires, Argentina. Because of their long migration, they are the latest species to arrive for the Pacific Northwest nesting season, with most arriving in early June. In August, flocks of more than 100 birds form in preparation for their southward migration, with most departing the Northwest by the middle of September.

WHERE TO FIND COMMON NIGHTHAWKS

Although you'll find Common Nighthawks in the western parts of Oregon and Washington, they are more common east of the Cascade Crest. They are occasionally active during the day, but the best time to watch them in action is at dusk. Look for them near water where you find lots of flying insects. Listen for their unique calls. They are much more difficult to find when they are roosting; look for odd bumps on bare tree limbs or wooden fences.

In Washington

Wenas Lake near Yakima

Mount Constitution on Orcas Island

Trout Lake Natural Area Preserve near Trout
Lake

Toppenish National Wildlife Refuge near
Yakima

In Oregon

Metolius Preserve and Metolius River trails
near Camp Sherman

Klamath Marsh National Wildlife Refuge near
Klamath Falls

Crane Prairie Reservoir near La Pine

Whitehorse Park near Grants Pass

OTHER BIRDS TO SEE

As dusk falls on a streamside forest east of the
Cascades, the air quickly cools and all kinds of
creatures take to the air. The ubiquitous mosquitoes are followed by their predators, the VIOLET-
GREEN SWALLOWS that are almost ready to
roost for the night and the bats that are just
waking up. The whinny of a Western Screech
Owl carries through the trees, and the large
shadow of a GREAT HORNED OWL passes over.

OLIVE-SIDED FLYCATCHER

Contopus cooperi

PERHAPS IT'S WISHFUL thinking that turns the three-note song of this flycatcher into "Quick, THREE beers!", but once you make the association, you'll know this birdsong for life. Olive-sided Flycatchers emit their loud, unmistakable song with the enthusiasm of a spirited bar patron, but you'll often hear the song without being able to locate the singer.

The Olive-sided Flycatcher hunts from high, exposed perches, giving you a good opportunity to look for field marks. Its dapper vest and upright posture make it unique. The Western Wood-Pewee is another large flycatcher, but it is smudgy looking and lacks the crisp, dark vest and the white belly and chin of the Olive-sided.

FOOD AND FORAGING

Olive-sided Flycatchers perch prominently on exposed branches at or near the tops of trees. From this perch, they scan the top story of a forest opening for bees and other flying insects. When an insect is spotted, the bird darts out in a quick burst of flight, catches the insect with a snap of its bill, and returns to its perch. It swallows small prey, such as flying ants, in flight, but brings larger prey, such as a bumblebees or moths, back to the perch and beats the creature against the branch to make it easier to swallow.

PAIRING AND PARENTING

In tall conifers such as Douglas-firs, hemlocks, and spruces, the female constructs a cup-shaped nest and incubates three or four eggs for about 15 days. Both parents capture insects and deliver them to nestlings during the 20 days they are in the nest and for at least two weeks after they leave.

MIGRATIONS AND MOVEMENTS

This world-traveler has the longest migratory path of any Northwest flycatcher. Individuals spend the winter in Panama and South America, and most arrive to nest in the Northwest during the month of May. Nesting begins in June, and by the end of August most birds have departed from the region, heading back to Central and South America.

WHERE TO FIND OLIVE-SIDED FLYCATCHERS

Look for them in coniferous forests of Oregon and Washington. Open areas within forests provide excellent foraging habitat. You will likely hear one before you see it; scan for an upright bird on an exposed perch.

In Washington

Mount Rainier National Park

English Camp on San Juan Island

Bethel Ridge Road (Forest Service Road 1500) off Highway 12 near Naches

Discovery Park in Seattle

In Oregon

Pittock Mansion in Portland

Larch Mountain near Troutdale

Cold Springs Campground near Sisters

Mount Ashland near Ashland

OTHER BIRDS TO SEE

Forest openings created by clearcutting, fire, landslide, or windthrow provide an ideal habitat for an interesting variety of birds that move in to take advantage of the insect prey and elbow room. You might spot LAZULI BUNTINGS, Orange-crowned Warblers, White-crowned Sparrows, WESTERN BLUEBIRDS, and Gray Jays in this seemingly barren, yet rich, habitat.

CANYON WREN

Catherpes mexicanus

NOTHING SAYS "Welcome to canyon country!" like the song of a Canyon Wren. Its slurred whistles tumble downward like water over a rocky cliff. Its disproportionally large song echoes from nooks and crannies to fill canyons and cliff sides, cheerily entertaining hikers and climbers. The descending, whistled call may be all you get from the secretive bird, but it's enough to make a day in the dry country complete.

This rust-colored species with a brilliant white throat fits right into the rocky country with its warm color and wedged shape. Like other wrens, it sports a relatively long, needle-like bill that is slightly down-curved. The only similar bird in similar habitats is the Rock Wren, whose range completely overlaps that of the Canyon Wren. With gray upper parts and a buff-colored belly, Rock Wrens are more earth-toned than Canyon Wrens. Rock Wrens also lack the sharp contrast between the white throat and rusty back and belly that distinguishes the Canyon Wren.

FOOD AND FORAGING

Canyon Wrens are often heard before they are seen, because they are usually hidden from view in a rocky crevice, where they look for food such as spiders. Their short legs, long bills, and wedge-shaped heads are perfect for probing into narrow spaces to fetch a hiding invertebrate.

PAIRING AND PARENTING

Canyon Wrens hide their nests inside rocky outcroppings, in caves, or in spaces between small rocks or boulders. To keep the eggs and nestlings cozy in a space that sees no sun, pairs construct a bulky nest with a soft cup lined with moss, feathers, and hair. The female incubates the eggs for 16 days, while the male brings her food. The five to six nestlings remain in the nest for 18 days after hatching and are then dependent on their parents for another three weeks.

MIGRATIONS AND MOVEMENTS

They remain in Oregon and Washington throughout the year, but in winter some leave their rocky nesting sites for lower elevations or densely vegetated areas to escape cold weather and food shortages.

WHERE TO FIND CANYON WRENS

Look for them east of the Cascades, where they are associated with canyons, cliffs, and coulees or any appropriate rocky habitat. Hearing this bird's song is the best way to detect one as it works its way among the rocks.

In Washington

Cowiche Canyon near Yakima

Ginkgo Petrified Forest State Park near Ellensburg

Yakima Canyon near Yakima

Oak Creek Wildlife Area near Naches

In Oregon

Fort Rock State Park near La Pine

Smith Rock State Park near Redmond

Deschutes River State Park near The Dalles

The Cove Palisades State Park near Madras

OTHER BIRDS TO SEE

While you are listening for the elusive Canyon Wren, look for some more visible birds such as PRAIRIE FALCONS, Turkey Vultures, White-throated Swifts, VIOLET-GREEN SWALLOWS, Cliff Swallows, Say's Phoebes, and CALIFORNIA QUAIL.

PACIFIC WREN

Troglodytes pacificus

THE PACIFIC WREN more than compensates for its diminutive size with a prolonged, bubbly song that seems to spread throughout a damp forest, echoing off of every tree trunk and mossy rock. This happy song packs in more than 30 notes per second, which gives it a kinetic quality. The bird's scientific name means cave dweller of the Pacific, which seems apt for this secretive little wren.

This mouse-sized bird is solid brown with black barring on its wings, tail, and undersides. Bewick's Wrens and House Wrens are also found in wooded areas of the region. Both are larger with bills that are longer and more curved than that of the Pacific Wren. These three species can also be distinguished by relative tail length and the color of the stripe above their eyes. The Bewick's Wren has a very long tail and a white stripe, the House Wren has a

medium-sized tail and a buff-colored stripe, and the Pacific Wren has a stubby tail and a buff-colored stripe.

FOOD AND FORAGING

In search of insects, spiders, and other creepy crawlies hiding in crevices in a mature forest, Pacific Wrens creep and flit near streams and in upland areas. No areas in the lower levels of a forest go unsearched. They use their tiny bills to probe bark, fallen logs, leaf litter, mossy patches, and even streams for small prey. Berries and seeds also form a part of their diet.

PAIRING AND PARENTING

Males are manic nest builders and use a variety of nest designs. They build spherical nests in spaces such as old woodpecker cavities, upturned root wads, and along stream banks. A male may construct several of these nests each year. When a female is sufficiently impressed with his work, she selects a nest and indicates her approval by lining the interior with fine material. After lining a nest, the female lays five to seven eggs and incubates them for 16 days. Both adults bring insects, spiders, and the like to nestlings. The family group stays in the male's territory, where both parents will care for the young until they disperse in a few weeks.

MIGRATIONS AND MOVEMENTS

Pacific Wrens are found year-round in forests that experience mild winters. Males sing throughout the year but increase the frequency of singing in late winter and early spring. The long nesting season begins in April and ends in August. During this time, some females raise a second brood of young after the first has fledged. Some birds disperse from high-elevation forests in the winter and occupy shrubby habitats, such as low-elevation clearcuts and city parks, until it is time to return to the forest for the nesting season.

WHERE TO FIND PACIFIC WRENS

Look for them all year in the wet forests of the Northwest. Listen for its song and its sharp, repeated "chip!" from low perches such as stumps or downed logs.

In Washington

Point Defiance Park in Tacoma

Discovery Park in Seattle

Lake Quinault in the Olympic National Forest

Ridgefield National Wildlife Refuge, Carty Unit, near Vancouver

In Oregon

Audubon Society of Portland's Nature Sanctuary near Forest Park

Cape Perpetua Scenic Area near Yachats

Ecola State Park near Cannon Beach

Silver Falls State Park near Salem

OTHER BIRDS TO SEE

You don't have to wait for neotropical migrants to arrive to enjoy birdsong in the Pacific Northwest. Our resident birds start warming up as the days begin to lengthen and are in full voice by early April. Song Sparrows, Bewick's Wrens, Spotted Towhees, Purple Finches, BROWN CREEPERS, and Northern Flickers all get a jump on the spring season, and you can learn their songs and calls early, before the warblers, flycatchers, and vireos arrive to complicate things.

SWAINSON'S THRUSH

Catharus ustulatus

WITH BROWNISH COLORATION and an affinity for dense, shady vegetation, the Swainson's Thrush might be difficult for us to see, but it demands to be heard. When it's singing a melodious song or dipping into its repertoire of call notes, this bird will entrance you. Its all-day call note sounds a bit like a water drop, "wup!", but it will perform its impressive song most frequently at dawn and dusk. Spiraling upward through the trees, this otherworldly music is a perfect set of bookends for a summer day.

The Swainson's Thrush has soft brown spots on a light breast, and a brown tail that matches its back. When you are trying to identify one of the three species of brown thrushes that visit the Northwest, time of year and habitat are good indicators of which thrush you are viewing. The Hermit Thrush is the only species of spotted thrush that regularly spends the winter in our region, and in the summer it nests in high-elevation coniferous forests. West of the Cascades, the Swainson's Thrush is commonly found in low-elevation forests with a mixture of conifers and deciduous trees and shrubs. The Veery is found only east of the Cascades, at lower elevations than the Swainson's or Hermit Thrush, in thickets of deciduous shrubs.

FOOD AND FORAGING

Like other thrushes, the Swainson's switches from a diet of fruit in fall and winter to one of insects during the spring and summer. They forage higher in the forest layers than most other thrushes, capturing insects by darting from a perch like a flycatcher or a warbler.

PAIRING AND PARENTING

After pairing with a male, the female constructs a well-concealed nest from ground level to 10 feet high in a shrub or a tree. She incubates four eggs for at least ten days and broods nestlings to keep them warm until they develop their own insulating feathers. Both parents feed nestlings insects and fruit that is in season. Young leave the nest about twelve days after hatching and are independent from their parents two weeks later. At this time, they move to areas near streams and capture the abundant insects there.

MIGRATIONS AND MOVEMENTS

Swainson's Thrushes nest throughout forested portions of Oregon and Washington and depart the region by September to spend the winter in Mexico. Springtime migrants arrive in early May, and males begin singing near the end of the month. In September, waves of southbound migrants pass over our region at night. Astute birders can hear these nocturnal migrants as they call to one another in the darkness.

WHERE TO FIND SWAINSON'S THRUSHES

These operatic singers are found in forests all over the Northwest during the summer, but they are most abundant in low-elevation forests on the west side of the Cascades. Find them in deciduous forests in areas with lots of delicious berries.

In Washington

Moran State Park on Orcas Island

Point Defiance Park in Tacoma

Nisqually National Wildlife Refuge near Olympia

Marymoor Park in Redmond

In Oregon

Wildwood Recreation Site near Brightwood

Reehers Camp in the Tillamook State Forest

William L. Finley National Wildlife Refuge near Corvallis

Breitenbush Campground near Detroit

OTHER BIRDS TO SEE

In the late spring, the low- and mid-elevation forests west of the Cascades offer a symphony of birdsong. Joining the chorus are WILSON'S WARBLERS, BLACK-HEADED GROSBEAKS, RED-BREASTED NUTHATCHES, Pacific-slope Flycatchers, and Warbling Vireos.

VARIED THRUSH

Ixoreus naevius

Male Varied Thrush

THE BRIGHT ORANGE plumage of the Varied Thrush is the perfect color for getting attention in a dark Pacific forest, much to the chagrin of these shy ground dwellers that tend to flush and hide in a tree as soon as they are noticed by human eyes. This striking bird has an equally memorable song, whistling two notes simultaneously in harmony to create an eerie sound that seems to come from every direction at once.

The Varied Thrush is similar to the ubiquitous American Robin in shape and size, but its bright orange throat, head stripe, and wing bars distinguish it from all other birds. The sexes are most easily distinguished by the breast band, which is black on the male and gray-brown on the female.

FOOD AND FORAGING

During much of the year, Varied Thrushes take advantage of the abundance of berries that grow in the Pacific Northwest. They feast on native crops such as salmonberry, snowberry, and huckleberry, and they also eat cultivated fruits, such as blackberry and unharvested apples. This species also eats acorns and will visit a backyard feeder stocked with cracked corn and millet. During the nesting season, they consume ground-dwelling insects, which they find by tossing litter aside with their bills. When the breeding season nears its end and berries begin to ripen, they switch back to a fruit-heavy diet.

PAIRING AND PARENTING

Females build a rather elaborate nest with a base of small twigs, an inner layer of rotted wood and moss, a lining of fine material, and a decorative outer layer of green moss. These conspicuous nests are built in trees, from ground level to 60 feet high. The female incubates three or four eggs for 12 or more days. Both parents feed the nestlings, which leave the nest two weeks after hatching. In some areas, Varied Thrushes have a long nesting season and can successfully raise two broods of young per year.

MIGRATIONS AND MOVEMENTS

Varied Thrushes nesting in Canada and Alaska migrate south after the nesting season, and many nesting in the Lower 48 simply move to lower elevations. During colder winters, they are quite abundant in low-elevation valleys of Oregon and Washington. During mild winters, they may remain in their mid-elevation nesting areas. Wintering birds depart for their forested nesting grounds in April and return to Northwest valleys in September or October.

WHERE TO FIND VARIED THRUSHES

During the winter, you'll find them in mid-elevation forests all the way down to sea level. Because Varieds have to wait for areas in upper elevations to thaw before they migrate in the spring, you can often still hear them singing into June at low elevations. Head uphill to find them during the breeding season. They often forage along trails and roadsides, so watch for the flash of orange on their wings as they fly up to a safer perch. They sometimes visit feeders, eating the dropped seed on the ground beneath them.

In Washington

Hurricane Ridge in Olympic National Park (breeding)

Mount Rainier National Park (breeding)

Snoqualmie Pass on Interstate 90 (breeding)

Discovery Park in Seattle (winter)

In Oregon

Cape Meares State Park near Tillamook (winter)

Oxbow Regional Park near Troutdale (winter)

Ecola State Park near Cannon Beach (winter)

Crater Lake National Park (breeding)

OTHER BIRDS TO SEE

In addition to the usual cast of characters found in alpine forests of the Cascade Range, such as PILEATED WOODPECKERS, PACIFIC WRENS, and OLIVE-SIDED FLYCATCHERS, the high-elevation nesting sites of the Varied Thrush are also home to Clark's Nutcrackers, MOUNTAIN BLUEBIRDS, and RED CROSSBILLS.

Female Varied Thrush

BLACK-HEADED GROSBEAK

Pheucticus melanocephalus

Male
Black-headed
Grosbeak

BLACK-HEADED GROSBEAKS have one of the most melodic voices of the spring, singing sweet phrases from the treetops, while flying, or even while sitting on a nest. Males and females both sing, which is unusual in the world of birds. Their fast, creatively whistled song sounds like it's coming from a robin that's had singing lessons. Each warbling phrase is clear and perfectly in tune. Their thick, cardinal-like beaks look intimidating, but these birds are mild mannered and eat seeds, fruit, and invertebrates.

Like a ripe fruit decorating the branches of deciduous trees, the male's bright orange, black, and white plumage stands out against the summer greens or the blue sky. Black-headed Grosbeaks have the namesake black head and a bright orange belly. Females are a buff-color, with pale orange on the belly, a brown back, and striped head. Their large, conical bills give

the species a very different appearance from any other black and orange bird that you will find in the Northwest. Bullock's Orioles slightly resemble Black-headeds in that they are black, orange, and white, but Bullock's have thin, pointed beaks, and their heads are not entirely black. Evening Grosbeaks also have thick beaks, but their plumage is yellow, not orange, and neither sex has a black or striped head.

FOOD AND FORAGING

Black-headed Grosbeaks eat a variety of things throughout the year. Fleshy fruits, tiny seeds, and a variety of insects are always on the menu. They use their thick bills to crack the husks of seeds and exoskeletons of beetles. These strong-stomached foragers will even eat Monarch butterflies, which are toxic to most birds.

PAIRING AND PARENTING

Females quickly choose a mate upon arrival at the nesting grounds and begin constructing nests by the end of spring. Nests are located in shrubs or trees, usually near streams or other forest openings. The female constructs the nest, a fairly crude cup of twigs lined with fine material. In a behavior that seems to court danger, the male frequently sings while incubating the eggs. Young hatch after 13 days, and both parents feed the nestlings a combination of plant and insect matter. Young climb out of the nest 10 to 14 days after hatching, but they can't fly for another two weeks.

Female Black-headed Grosbeak

MIGRATIONS AND MOVEMENTS

Black-headeds spend the winter in Mexico and Central America and arrive in the Pacific Northwest in late April or early May. During the month of May, they are quite conspicuous, because males establish territories and begin singing in earnest. They are less visible in June and July, when they spend less time singing and more time raising their young. Males begin to leave the region in late July, most females depart in August, and the young stick around the longest, usually departing by mid-September.

WHERE TO FIND BLACK-HEADED GROSBEAKS

Look for them throughout Oregon and Washington during the breeding season, in appropriate low-elevation deciduous forest habitats. To find them, listen for their cheerful song or their "squik!" call. The bright colors of the male stand out in flight, so watch the trees. You can also find them at bird feeders all summer long, joined eventually by their fuzzy fledglings.

In Washington

Oak Creek Wildlife Area near Naches

Blackbird Island in Leavenworth

Marymoor Park in Redmond

Dungeness River Audubon Center in Sequim

In Oregon

Metolius Preserve and Metolius River trails near Camp Sherman

Tualatin Hills Nature Park in Beaverton

Beaver Creek State Natural Area near Newport

Bear Creek Greenway in Ashland

OTHER BIRDS TO SEE

Brightly colored birds abound at bird feeders during the summer. Joining the orange Black-headed Grosbeaks are the yellow American Goldfinches, the purple BAND-TAILED PIGEONS, the copper-colored RUFOUS HUMMINGBIRDS, and the red-spotted Hairy Woodpeckers.

WESTERN MEADOWLARK

Sturnella neglecta

SOUNDING A LITTLE like a squeaky wind instrument, the melodious song of a Western Meadowlark travels well across the expanses of grass and sagebrush; its song is emblematic of open spaces. Its bright plumage and irresistibly bubbly song have won it many admirers. In fact, six states, including Oregon, have adopted this grassland jewel as their state bird.

Western Meadowlarks have a bright yellow belly with a black V-shaped band across their chest. Their backs are brown and the edges of their tails are white. Their silhouette is distinctive, with a pointed beak, short neck, and

rounded belly, kind of like the Penguin in the Batman comics. Luckily for identification purposes, its doppelganger the Eastern Meadowlark isn't found in the Northwest, and no other bird really resembles it.

FOOD AND FORAGING

This species uses its lancelike bill to probe the ground and spread apart blades of grass to find seeds, insects, and spiders. It also plucks insects, such as grasshoppers, from grass or other low vegetation.

PAIRING AND PARENTING

At the start of the nesting season, males establish territories in grassy areas. A male might pair with one female and then add a second mate after the first begins incubating eggs. Within the territory, females select areas with tall grass and thick layers of dead plants to provide cover for their nests, which are built on the ground. Surrounding grass and other plant material is incorporated into an elaborate structure that features a domelike roof and a tunnel leading away from the nest. The female lays four or five eggs and incubates them for 14 days. Young stay in the nest for 10 to 12 days and are fed by the female and the male, unless he is busy tending another brood. Upon leaving the nest, fledglings can walk and run but are unable to fly for several more days.

MIGRATIONS AND MOVEMENTS

During fall and winter, Western Meadowlarks travel in flocks that can exceed 100 individuals. In the winter, they leave the central and eastern portions of Oregon and Washington, and many move to the coasts and western valleys. Males begin singing in March or April to kick off the nesting season.

WHERE TO FIND WESTERN MEADOWLARKS

Western Meadowlarks can show up about anywhere in Oregon or Washington outside of the mountains. They are more common west of the Cascades during the winter, but they are abundant on the east side during the spring and summer. Their mottled brown backs render them virtually invisible in the grass, so look for them perched on fences or power lines, flaunting their bright yellow bellies. If you see a chunky brown bird flying away from you, look for the telltale white edges on the tail.

In Washington

Conboy Lake National Wildlife Refuge near Glenwood

Skagit Wildlife Area near Mount Vernon

Marymoor Park in Redmond

Toppenish National Wildlife Refuge near Yakima

In Oregon

TouVelle State Park near Medford

William L. Finley National Wildlife Refuge near Corvallis

Powell Butte Nature Park in Portland

Hatfield Lake near Bend

OTHER BIRDS TO SEE

Although they might not look it, Western Meadowlarks are members of the blackbird family, which is known for bright colors and lots of noise. During the summer, the Northwest is full of blackbirds, including Bullock's Orioles, Brewer's Blackbirds, Red-winged Blackbirds, YELLOW-HEADED BLACKBIRDS, and Brown-headed Cowbirds.

Tree Trunk Birds
LIVING THE VERTICAL LIFE

AMONG THE EMBLEMS of the Pacific Northwest are its trees—really big trees. Douglas-fir, Sitka spruce, Ponderosa pine, and a variety of others color the landscape and provide wonderful places for woodpeckers, nuthatches, and creepers to find food and shelter. These tree trunk birds depend heavily on live trees and standing dead trees, or snags. Although these birds may appear superficially similar, each has evolved unique methods of obtaining resources from our treasured forests.

We have chosen a collection of our favorite woodpeckers—those that are the most fun to watch and that live in beautiful places. These birds are often the highlight of bird walks that we lead and capture the interest of even a reluctant birder with their charisma. Some of these woodpeckers inhabit forests throughout the region, and others are confined to dry forests east of the Cascade Crest. The wonderful thing about this group of woodpeckers is that each species has distinct markings, and you need only one good look to identify any one of them.

Woodpeckers are easily recognized by their vertical posture and pointed bill, which they use to excavate nest cavities, capture prey, and rap loudly, or drum, on a surface to announce their presence. A pile of woodchips at the base of a tree is evidence that a pair of woodpeckers has recently excavated a nesting cavity. When the parents have finished excavating, the female lays eggs on the bare cavity floor and both parents share incubation duties. A few weeks after hatching, woodpecker nestlings beg loudly for food. If you hear muffled squawking emanating from a tree trunk, find a good hiding place several yards away from the tree—so as not to disturb the parents—and you will soon be rewarded by the sight of one or two woodpeckers arriving with food.

Red-breasted Nuthatches and Brown Creepers resemble woodpeckers in some ways but are songbirds and are distinguished by their own adaptations to the vertical life. The Red-breasted Nuthatch is the most common and most colorful of the three nuthatch species found in the Pacific Northwest. The Brown Creeper is the only species of creeper found in North America and is therefore very easy to identify. Learning about these fascinating species, most of which inhabit our area year-round, will add another dimension to your enjoyment of the Northwest's forests.

LEWIS'S WOODPECKER

Melanerpes lewis

AS YOU WALK into an oak woodland, you see a dark bird swoop out to capture a wasp in mid-air. Another bird drops to the ground and then returns to a branch with a grasshopper in its bill. This relentless predator of insects hovers in the air to snatch up anything that moves. When you find the perched bird in your binoculars, you see a red face, pink belly, and gray nape. You notice that the dark wings and back are actually a glossy green. These are not crows, flycatchers, or swallows, but Lewis's Woodpeckers. A dozen species of woodpeckers are found in the Northwest, but the Lewis's looks and behaves like none other. Do not pass up a chance to visit one of the few sites where you can spot this striking bird.

When Meriwether Lewis first described this bird, he thought it might be a crow—an easy mistake to make. Lewis's Woodpeckers appear solid black from a distance, but you can easily distinguish them from crows by the pink feathers on their bellies and the pale feathers around their necks. Unlike most woodpeckers, they often perch upright on branches instead of clinging vertically to tree trunks.

FOOD AND FORAGING

The Lewis's Woodpecker's diet changes with the seasons, and its foraging techniques are unusual among woodpeckers. During the summer, it catches insects in the air or off the ground but doesn't search for insects by boring into trees. During the nonbreeding season, it consumes acorns, grains, and fruits, which it stores in crevices of trees to retrieve during the lean winter months.

PAIRING AND PARENTING

Lewis's Woodpeckers rarely excavate their own nest cavities, once again defying the woodpecker stereotype. Instead, they use cavities created by other woodpeckers or nest boxes constructed by helpful humans. Five to nine eggs are incubated for 12 to 16 days. Both parents feed insects to the nestlings during their monthlong stay in the nest.

MIGRATIONS AND MOVEMENTS

In areas with enough oaks to provide ample acorns for the winter, Lewis's Woodpeckers will remain year-round. Birds that breed in pine forests migrate to lower elevations or latitudes in the fall and form nomadic flocks in search of food. Males establish territories on their nesting grounds and begin courting females in April or May. The nesting season ends when young leave the nest in July or August.

WHERE TO FIND LEWIS'S WOODPECKERS

You'll find Lewis's in burned pine forests, oak or cottonwood woodlands, or areas where pine forests transitions to shrub land. Look for their dark forms on leafless branches of large trees. Their fly-catching behavior is also very conspicuous and will immediately alert you to their presence. During the summer, listen for their squeaky wheel call. When searching burned pine forests, look for areas where only large trees remain with open space between them. Such places are ideal for Lewis's Woodpeckers hunting aerial and terrestrial insects.

In Washington

Fort Simcoe State Park near Toppenish (year-round)

Oak Creek Wildlife Area near Naches (year-round)

In Oregon

Tygh Valley area along Highway 197 (year-round)

Burned areas near Sisters and Bend (May through August)

Cabin Lake Campground near Fort Rock (May through August)

OTHER BIRDS TO SEE

In deciduous woodlands, you might spot ACORN WOODPECKERS, White-breasted Nuthatches, WESTERN BLUEBIRDS, and American Kestrels. In burned forests, marvel at the large number of cavity-nesting species that take advantage of the abundant insects and weakened trees. Look for BLACK-BACKED WOODPECKERS, Hairy Woodpeckers, House Wrens, and WESTERN BLUEBIRDS.

ACORN WOODPECKER

Melanerpes formicivorus

WITH THEIR CLOWNISH faces, cartoonish calls, and acorn-stashing antics, these birds radiate personality. Watching a group of Acorn Woodpeckers as they harvest acorns and deliberate over the perfect spots to place them in a granary tree is a wonderful way to spend a fall day. With social lives that could inspire a soap opera, these birds have kept ornithologists perplexed for decades.

The white patches on its wings and rump in flight contrast with its black back and catch your attention. Upon closer inspection, you'll see its yellow face, which is unmistakable, as are its red cap and pale iris. Its memorable laughing call, reminiscent of Woody Woodpecker, also distinguishes it from other woodpeckers of the area.

FOOD AND FORAGING

Acorn Woodpeckers have a diverse diet that includes acorns, insects, tree sap, and fruit. Acorns, which are low in nutrients and high in tannins, are not their optimal food (which is insects) but are an essential supplement when other foods are not available. They harvest acorns from oaks and bring them either to an anvil site for immediate opening and consumption or to a granary for storage. They usually construct granaries in the trunks of snags, but Acorn Woodpeckers will also create holes in dead branches of live trees or even in telephone poles. Each hole is custom-made for an individual acorn, and the builder takes care to ensure a snug fit before moving on to the next one.

PAIRING AND PARENTING

Acorn Woodpecker granary in a Ponderosa pine

On today's episode of The Young and the Crestless: Who are the nestlings' true parents? What does that mysterious male hanging around the nest want? Tune in to find out.

In most bird species, a pair of adults shares the duties of raising the young. Most Acorn Woodpeckers, however, nest in groups, not pairs, with up to 13 birds sharing the duties at a single nest! Both males and females excavate the nest cavity in a dead tree, incubate the eggs, and feed the young. Eggs of multiple females can be laid in one nest, with all the mothers chipping in to help with the young. Nonparental helpers assist with incubation and feeding duties while they await a vacancy in the reproductive ranks of the group. This information comes from a well-studied population of Acorn Woodpeckers in California, but similar social behavior occurs in the Northwest.

MIGRATIONS AND MOVEMENTS

Most Acorn Woodpeckers remain in their territories year-round. In places or times when the acorn crop fails, groups migrate to find more dependable food sources. They have a very long nesting season, because groups may raise multiple broods of young between May and September. In late summer, when adults are no longer feeding nestlings, they begin to harvest acorns for storage in their granaries.

WHERE TO FIND ACORN WOODPECKERS

Sites where Acorn Woodpeckers are found throughout the year have lots of oaks, including ornamental species, and some snags for use as granaries. As you walk in an area full of oaks, look for granary trees that are peppered with acorn holes. Acorn Woodpecker groups are easily located by their social chattering, and individuals are very visible as they flash their white wing patches in flight. Because they nest and forage in groups, you will often find several more birds after you locate the first.

In Washington

Not common, but sometimes found around Balch Lake near Lyle

In Oregon

Dawson Creek Corporate Park in Hillsboro (in snags along the creek itself)

William L. Finley National Wildlife Refuge near Corvallis (headquarters)

TouVelle State Park near Medford (trail that begins at the last parking area)

Emigrant Lake County Park and other natural areas in or near Ashland

OTHER BIRDS TO SEE

Oak trees feed a variety of birds with the acorns they grow and the insects they attract. As you're viewing Acorn Woodpeckers, watch for White-breasted Nuthatches, Western Scrub-Jays, LEWIS'S WOODPECKERS, and WOOD DUCKS.

WILLIAMSON'S SAPSUCKER

Sphyrapicus thyroideus

Male Williamson's Sapsucker

OVER THE SOUND of a bubbling creek, you hear a slow drumming from high on the trunk of a pine tree. Patient searching finally reveals the flashy pattern of stripes and splotches on a male Williamson's Sapsucker. Uncommon and secretive, this species is an elusive prize for those seeking their 12-woodpecker grand slam in the Northwest. It was a puzzle to those who first discovered it as well; the dissimilar brightly striped male and camouflaged brown-black female specimens were assigned to different species for 16 years until someone finally saw a nesting pair and figured it out.

These birds show dramatic sexual dimorphism, meaning that males and females have different plumage. Most woodpeckers show subtle differences between males and females, such as the presence or absence of a small red spot, but Williamson's Sapsuckers are dramatically different. Females are drab, with brown heads, yellow bellies, and barring on their backs. The males are strikingly marked with a red chin, yellow belly, white wing patches and facial stripes, and a solid black back.

FOOD AND FORAGING

Williamson's are omnivorous and change their diet during the year depending on what food is most abundant. As their name suggests, they drink sap from small cavities that they carve into the trunks of coniferous trees. They frequently tend these wells to keep them flowing and consume any insects attracted to the sap. In spring and early summer, the adults' diet consists completely of the sap and inner bark of coniferous trees. During the nesting season, adults and young add ants and other insects to their diet.

PAIRING AND PARENTING

Although they forage on conifers, Williamson's Sapsuckers often nest in aspen groves. They prefer the softness of dead or live-but-rotting trees for cavity sites, because these birds are weaker excavators than some other woodpecker species. Males perform most of the cavity excavation work, and females lay four to six eggs, which are incubated by both parents for 13 days. Young leave the nest one month after hatching.

MIGRATIONS AND MOVEMENTS

Most Northwest populations of Williamson's Sapsucker are migratory, leaving for California and Mexico by October. They return to the Northwest in March and April, as the sap begins to flow. Males establish territories prior to the arrival of females at the nesting grounds. The nesting season lasts from May to late June or early July when young have left the nest.

WHERE TO FIND WILLIAMSON'S SAPSUCKERS

Female Williamson's Sapsucker

Look for them in pine and mixed conifer forests east of the Cascades in both Oregon and Washington. From May through July, focus your search on groves of aspens that are surrounded by coniferous forest. Williamson's Sapsuckers can be difficult to find, but a bird will announce

its presence with a distinctive drawn-out drum. It sounds something like "Rat-a-tatat, rat-a-tat, tat-tat, tat-tat."

In Washington

Bethel Ridge Road (Forest Service Road 1500) off Highway 12 near Naches

In Oregon

Shevlin Park near Bend

Cold Springs Campground near Sisters

Calliope Crossing near Sisters

OTHER BIRDS TO SEE

Aspen groves can be a nest-finding bonanza in the spring. You might find the less elusive (but still interesting) Red-naped Sapsucker nesting nearby. Many other birds will nest in sapsucker cavities in future years, including VIOLET-GREEN SWALLOWS, Northern Pygmy Owls, and House Wrens.

RED-BREASTED SAPSUCKER

Sphyrapicus ruber

THIS BRIGHT DENIZEN of western forests is a delight to watch as it plucks elderberries or flies from tree to tree like a like a ruby-tipped dart. Orderly rows of sap wells decorate the tree trunks in its territory. Catching a glimpse of this small, flashy woodpecker is easy, because it moves around busily and doesn't seem to mind human company. The sight of a Red-breasted Sapsucker's red head, juxtaposed against a mossy green background, enlivens any walk in the woods.

Although it does indeed have a red breast, Red-headed Sapsucker might have been a more descriptive name for this bird. The only similar species is the Red-naped Sapsucker, with which it sometimes interbreeds. The Red-breasted is differentiated from the Red-naped by the former's bright red head and breast that are not interrupted by white and black stripes. A Red-breasted Sapsucker has white wing patches, similar to other sapsuckers, but a careful look at its head will quickly let you know which species you've spotted.

FOOD AND FORAGING

Red-breasted Sapsuckers carve pea-sized sap wells in a variety of tree species and return to drink from them repeatedly. When Red-breasteds aren't looking, hummingbirds and other animals will visit the sap wells to steal a sugary sip. Ants are a favorite food of sapsuckers, and they also eat insects captured in midair.

PAIRING AND PARENTING

West of the Cascade Crest, Red-breasted Sapsuckers prefer large, dead trees for their nest cavities. Birds nesting east of the crest will excavate cavities in live trees, such as aspen, that are softened by fungal rot. Their incubation and nesting behaviors follow the usual patterns for woodpeckers, with males and females sharing the excavation, incubation, and feeding duties. Four to seven eggs are incubated for 11 to 14 days. Young leave the nest at about 24 days after hatching.

MIGRATIONS AND MOVEMENTS

In areas with mild climates such as western Oregon and Washington, Red-breasted Sapsuckers are present throughout the year. Pairs nest from May through July and care for their young for at least one week after they leave the nest. Individuals then disperse to find food for the fall and winter.

WHERE TO FIND RED-BREASTED SAPSUCKERS

Good news: Red-breasted Sapsuckers are widespread west of the Cascades, and you'll find them in just about any area with a mix of conifers and deciduous trees. Arboretums and landscaped parks with nonnative trees such as sugar maples are very popular with this species. Check the trunks of trees for horizontal rows of sap wells; the seeping ones are telltale signs that these birds are in the area. Listen for their whiny "nyeeah" calls and slow, erratic drumming. If you spot one in flight, its solid red head and white wing patches are unmistakable.

In Washington

Lake Sammamish State Park near Issaquah

Scatter Creek Wildlife Area near Olympia

Point No Point Lighthouse and County Park
  near Kingston

In Oregon

Forest Park in Portland

Calliope Crossing near Sisters

Rocky Point on Upper Klamath Lake

OTHER BIRDS TO SEE

Forests west of the Cascade Crest are full of must-see birds, especially during the breeding season. Watch and listen for BAND-TAILED PIGEONS, BROWN CREEPERS, RED-BREASTED NUTHATCHES, PILEATED WOODPECKERS, GREAT HORNED OWLS, OLIVE-SIDED FLY-CATCHERS, BUSHTITS, PACIFIC WRENS, VAR-IED THRUSHES, TOWNSEND'S WARBLERS, WILSON'S WARBLERS, WESTERN TANAGERS, and BLACK-HEADED GROSBEAKS.

WHITE-HEADED WOODPECKER

Picoides albolarvatus

Male
White-headed
Woodpecker

OPPOSITE:
Female
White-headed
Woodpecker

THE TOASTED BUTTERSCOTCH smell of giant Ponderosa pines fills the air, and electric green lichens light up sooty tree trunks. Sharp calls ring through the forest as a pair of White-headed Woodpeckers moves from tree to tree. Their white faces and dark eyes give them a cute and friendly appearance, kind of like small, feathered mimes. They seem to seek attention as they flash their white wing patches and land low in trees. Watch them for a while as they work their way up and down the huge pines, gleaning insects from every surface. Catching a glimpse of a White-headed Woodpecker is always exciting, because they are uncommon and are found only in a few pine forests in the western states.

Their name really says it all. This is the only woodpecker with a solid white face, although the back of its head is actually black. Males have a small red spot at the back of their crown and juveniles have a spot at the top of their head. The bird is otherwise solid black, except for white wing patches that are conspicuous in flight.

FOOD AND FORAGING

Ponderosa pines are the year-round pantry of the White-headed Woodpecker in much of its range. When the summer sun heats the pines, insects on the trunks and branches become active, making them easier for birds to find. When insect activity slows down during the fall and winter, pine seeds become a large part of the birds' diet. As spring approaches and the seed crop runs low, White-headed Woodpeckers carve sap wells in medium-sized pines, usually on the southwestern side of the trees, where the sun's warmth increases the flow.

PAIRING AND PARENTING

Although Ponderosa pines are essential for feeding, this species will nest in any tree that is soft enough for them to excavate a cavity. Nest construction takes more than three weeks, a long time for a bird. After a 14-day incubation period, both parents bring insects to feed their four or five nestlings during the 26 days they inhabit the nest.

MIGRATIONS AND MOVEMENTS

White-headed Woodpeckers are nonmigratory, because pines provide them with a year-round

food source. Pairs begin nest construction in May, and young leave the nest in June or July. Some individuals remain in the nesting area throughout the year, but others disperse after nesting and return in the spring.

WHERE TO FIND WHITE-HEADED WOODPECKERS

Although White-headed Woodpeckers are found in the Pacific Northwest year-round, they're most often seen during the nesting season. Look for them in Ponderosa pine forests along the east side of the Cascades and in dry forests in other ranges. They prefer areas with large trees and openings in the canopy where sun shines through to warm up the bark and get the insects moving. In summer, listen for their three-note rattling calls and watch for the flash of their wings as they fly from tree to tree. In winter, check the ends of branches for White-headeds feeding on the seeds inside the large, prickly pinecones; in spring, look for them feeding on sap from wells they've drilled in pine trunks.

In Washington

Leavenworth National Fish Hatchery near Leavenworth

Wenas Campground (Audubon Campground) near Ellensburg (rough road)

In Oregon

Cold Springs Campground near Sisters

Metolius Preserve and Metolius River trails near Camp Sherman

Cabin Lake Campground near Fort Rock

Mount Ashland near Ashland

OTHER BIRDS TO SEE

Look for other Ponderosa pine forest birds such as Pinyon Jays (Oregon only), Pygmy Nuthatches, RED CROSSBILLS, WILLIAMSON'S SAPSUCKERS, and BLACK-BACKED WOODPECKERS.

BLACK-BACKED WOODPECKER

Picoides arcticus

BLACK-BACKED WOODPECKERS are vagabonds in search of the next good place to find beetle larvae. They make a living eating the insects that infest severely burned trees, a great example of how wildfires can be beneficial. They thrive in burned forests, where their dark plumage blends perfectly with charred tree trunks. Black-backed Woodpeckers are all business as they attack an infested tree like a demolition crew. Industrious and persistent, they will often ignore you when they are in the middle of excavating. This behavior makes them very easy to watch.

Males sport a jaunty yellow cap, and both sexes have black backs, barred sides, and lack white wing patches. Hairy Woodpeckers look similar but have white on their backs. Three-toed Woodpeckers also have yellow caps, but their backs are barred.

FOOD AND FORAGING

Male
Black-backed
Woodpecker

Many woodpeckers take advantage of the influx of insects into burned forests, but Black-backeds are the most reliant on these wildfire sites and the beetles they attract. The beetles, which are also wildfire specialists, can detect smoke from 50 miles away and find fires using infrared vision. Black-backeds find the nutrient-rich beetle larvae by prying off bark and excavating the tunnels that the beetles have bored into the burned trunks.

PAIRING AND PARENTING

Black-backed Woodpeckers excavate most of their nests in snags, but, like other woodpeckers, they will also use live trees that have been softened by heart rot. Their cavity entrances slant upward with a beveled bottom edge, which can help you identify the makers of these holes. Parents take turns incubating three or four eggs during a 14-day period. During their 24-day stay in the nest, nestlings are fed a diet heavy in beetles by both parents.

MIGRATIONS AND MOVEMENTS

These nomads follow the fires and the food wherever it takes them. They might stay in one place for years or travel in any direction or elevation, regardless of the season. Pairs nest during the spring and summer months to take advantage of the peak insect activity.

WHERE TO FIND BLACK-BACKED WOODPECKERS

This species is not common, but if you look in the appropriate kind of habitat, your chances of seeing one are pretty good. Look for recently burned (five years ago or less) forests east of the Cascade Crest. Check Forest Service district offices, such as the one in Sisters, Oregon, for information about the latest burns and recent woodpecker sightings.

Listen for the persistent pecking of a foraging Black-backed. Look for burned tree trunks with chipped off bark where woodpeckers have been foraging. If you listen carefully, you might hear wood-boring beetles, this birds' primary food, chewing under the bark. Nesting season in May, June, or July is a peak of activity.

In Washington

Bethel Ridge Road (Forest Service Road 1500) off Highway 12 near Naches

In Oregon

Black Butte area near Sisters

Burned areas on Mount Hood (check with the ranger station in Parkdale)

OTHER BIRDS TO SEE

By attracting insects and creating new nest sites, wildfires provide habitat for a variety of birds. While you're looking for Black-backed Woodpeckers, you might also find OLIVE-SIDED FLYCATCHERS, WESTERN BLUEBIRDS, LAZULI BUNTINGS, TOWNSEND'S SOLITAIRES, and LEWIS'S WOODPECKERS.

PILEATED WOODPECKER

Dryocopus pileatus

Male Pileated
Woodpecker
with nestling

A HAUNTING CALL echoes through an ancient stand of Douglas-fir. You feel it resonate in your chest, and goose bumps rise on your arms. Woodchips rain down as a Pileated Woodpecker drives its large, pointed bill into a snag. A pointed red crest and yellow eyes give this bird a wild look, especially when it stops its work to turn and look at you. This awe-inspiring bird is not only a privilege to observe, but it also plays an important role in creating habitat for many forest animals.

The Pileated is the largest woodpecker in North America, depending on what you believe about the veracity of the recent sightings of the Ivory-billed Woodpecker, an even larger bird that was thought to be extinct. The Pileated's pointed red crest gives it a silhouette unique among Northwest woodpeckers. When it flies, white wing patches and underwing feathers contrast with its black body.

FOOD AND FORAGING

These big birds eat very small things. They create characteristic rectangular holes in tree trunks, often near the ground, while searching for ants and beetle larvae. Carpenter ants make up the bulk of their diet, but they will capitalize on the occasional beetle outbreak. Pileateds are the only woodpeckers that dig deep into the heartwood of trees. This trait is significant, because it creates foraging opportunities for other woodpecker species and spreads the fungal spores that cause heart rot, softening the wood for later excavation.

PAIRING AND PARENTING

Pileateds carve spacious nest cavities high in tall trees. Like other woodpeckers, they excavate a cavity but do not line it with nesting material. Instead, they lay eggs directly on the woody floor. They usually choose live trees for nesting and use a cavity only once, leaving important nesting and roosting sites for ducks, raptors, and other birds and mammals. Pileateds are the only woodpecker large enough and strong enough to make such wide holes in sturdy trees, earning them distinction as a keystone species, because of the significant effect they have on the entire ecosystem. Females lay an average of four eggs, which are incubated for 15 to 18 days. Pileated nestlings get quite large before they leave the nest one month after hatching. If you are lucky enough to find an active nest, you'll see nestlings poke their heads out of the cavity to grab a gulp of regurgitated ants brought by their parents.

Tree excavations created by a foraging Pileated Woodpecker

MIGRATIONS AND MOVEMENTS

Pileated Woodpeckers remain in the Pacific Northwest throughout the year. To escape the rough winter weather, they roost in the hollow interiors of decayed snags. They excavate multiple holes in the snag so that a back door is always available for escaping from danger. Pairs begin excavating nests in March or April, and the young leave the nest by the middle of July.

WHERE TO FIND PILEATED WOODPECKERS

Widespread across Oregon and Washington, their territories are quite large, so finding a Pileated is not always easy. Look for large, rectangular excavations in a large tree or log. Fresh woodchips scattered on the ground below are always a good sign. Although nest sites are high in trees, feeding sites can be very close to the ground, or even on the ground, so don't be surprised if you come around a corner to find

a Pileated at eye level or lower. Listen for its unmistakable "kek-kek-kek-kek" call, which is audible from great distances.

In Washington

Discovery Park in Seattle

Lake Wenatchee State Park near Wenatchee

Nisqually National Wildlife Refuge near Olympia

In Oregon

Forest Park in Portland

Tryon Creek State Park in Portland

Tualatin Hills Nature Park in Beaverton

William L. Finley National Wildlife Refuge near Corvallis

OTHER BIRDS TO SEE

Scan the trees for the bright colors of TOWNSEND'S WARBLERS and RED-BREASTED SAPSUCKERS. Listen for the sweet sounds of Purple Finches and PACIFIC WRENS. Get scolded by an orange-bellied Douglas' Squirrel popping out of an old Pileated Woodpecker cavity.

RED-BREASTED NUTHATCH

Sitta canadensis

THESE LIVELY, CHATTY birds are fun to watch as they take seeds from a feeder or explore the branches of a large tree. Like miniature woodpeckers, they glean insects from tree trunks and carve their own nest cavities. Unlike woodpeckers, they can move down a tree headfirst and lack long tails for bracing themselves against the trunk.

Nuthatches have a distinctive silhouette, appearing neckless with short, stubby tails. The black line that runs through their eye and contrasting white supercilium, or eyebrow, distinguish the Red-breasted from other nuthatches. Despite its name, the bird's breast is not truly red in color—its belly and breast are closer to orange. Males are slightly darker than females.

FOOD AND FORAGING

Nuthatches are so named because of this bird family's habit of putting a seed (or nut) in a crevice to hold it in place and using its chisel-like beak to break it open (or hatch it). Red-breasted Nuthatches feed primarily on seeds during the winter, and they are faithful visitors to bird feeders. They also look for beetles and other arthropods on the bark, needles, tops, and undersides of tree branches. No part of a tree is off limits to a hungry Red-breasted.

PAIRING AND PARENTING

Like woodpeckers, Red-breasted Nuthatches excavate nest cavities in rotting trees, but that is where the similarities end. Males begin digging several cavities, and the female chooses one and completes construction. She then brings in fur and fine plant material to line the cavity for the nest. This is the only North American species known to finish its nest by smearing sap around the entrance, sometimes using a piece of bark as a spatula. The stickiness of the sap seems to keep insects, other birds, and mammals from entering the nest cavity. Although the male does not incubate, he contributes by bringing food to the female, allowing her to stay on the nest and keep her six eggs at an optimum temperature during the 12-day incubation period. Both parents feed invertebrates to the nestlings until they fledge, about 20 days after hatching.

MIGRATIONS AND MOVEMENTS

These year-round Northwest residents are found in forests throughout the area during the spring and summer nesting season, but their winter movements are irregular, with some birds leaving their nesting grounds during some years to find new seed crops and bird feeders.

WHERE TO FIND RED-BREASTED NUTHATCHES

Conifer trees such as Douglas-firs are the best places to find Red-breasteds. They aren't confined to undisturbed wilderness—any forest, park, or back yard with large conifers will do. The abundance of this habitat in the Pacific Northwest makes it unnecessary to list specific sites. The easiest way to find a Red-breasted Nuthatch in the winter is to put up a suet or sunflower seed feeder. In the spring and summer, find a grove of large conifers and listen. Soon you should hear the repeated nasal "henk" of a male. The cadence of its call is similar to the slow beeps of a truck's backup alert.

OTHER BIRDS TO SEE

During the breeding season, forests in the Pacific Northwest are alive with birdsong. Listen for SWAINSON'S THRUSHES, WINTER WRENS, WESTERN TANAGERS, BLACK-HEADED GROSBEAKS, and WILSON'S WARBLERS. In the winter, Red-breasted Nuthatches join mixed-species flocks to share the burden of watching for predators. You might find them in the company of TOWNSEND'S WARBLERS, BROWN CREEPERS, Downy Woodpeckers, chickadees, and Golden-crowned Kinglets.

BROWN CREEPER

Certhia americana

BROWN CREEPERS ARE a spider's worst nightmare. First, the birds take spiderwebs for nest material, and then they return to eat the spiders themselves. Although these tiny birds can be difficult to see, they are easy to identify. They seem to play peek-a-boo with you as they circle a tree while you try to find them in your binoculars. Their cheery, enthusiastic song brightens the mood in a dark forest.

With their long, stiff tails and tree-climbing ability, Brown Creepers superficially resemble woodpeckers. Their needlelike decurved (downwardly curved) bill, however, is distinctive. With mottled backs of buff and brown, they blend perfectly with tree bark, which makes them difficult to see.

FOOD AND FORAGING

Brown Creepers' bills are ideal for plucking spiders and insects from furrows in tree bark. They begin foraging at the base of a tree and spiral their way up and around the trunk,

systematically probing the bark in search of food. After reaching the large upper branches, they fly down to the base of the next tree to repeat the process.

PAIRING AND PARENTING

Brown Creeper nests are gravity-defying marvels of adhesion. Somehow, this small bird manages to make a large, sturdy nest in a very precarious location. The female builds a base of coarse bark and twigs, and then lines the nest cup with collected hair and moss. The nest is sandwiched between the trunk of a tree and a large, partially detached section of bark. Spiderwebs and sticky insect cocoons are brought in to secure the nest material to the hanging bark. The female incubates five or six eggs for 15 days. After the eggs hatch, adults slip behind the bark to feed spiders and insects to the young during the 15-day nestling period.

MIGRATIONS AND MOVEMENTS

You can find Brown Creepers year-round in the Pacific Northwest. They leave high-elevation forests in the winter, when it is too cold to find their insect prey. Females begin constructing nests in April or May, depending on the weather. Young leave the nest in May, June, or July and roost together at night on the bark of trees for a few weeks before dispersing to find their own territories.

WHERE TO FIND BROWN CREEPERS

Large trees of any kind can attract Brown Creepers, but you are most likely to find them in mature conifer forests. Deciduous trees such as bigleaf maples, ashes, and alders also offer

A perfect
Brown Creeper
nest site

good habitat. You might hear its high, thin call or its "Trees! Trees! Beautiful trees!" song before you spot the bird itself. As you're trying to focus on one as it spirals upward on a tree, be patient and keep scanning. Eventually it will show itself when it flies down to the base of the next tree.

OTHER BIRDS TO SEE

As you watch Brown Creepers working the bark of large trees, you might also see RED-BREASTED NUTHATCHES, RED-BREASTED SAPSUCKERS, Hairy Woodpeckers, and Bewick's Wrens.

Urban Birds
MAKING A LIVING IN THE BIG CITY

THE URBAN AND SUBURBAN worlds present both problems and opportunities for wild birds. Windows, giant radio antennas, and cats injure and kill many birds passing through our cities. Fortunately, some aspects of our built environment benefit birds by providing sturdy structures on which to nest, insects and nectar to eat, and safe places to sleep during migration. Seattle, Portland, and other Northwest cities are particularly attractive to birds, thanks to abundant waterways, forested parks, and local efforts to protect and restore natural areas. Birders can hardly ask for a better place to live.

More than 100 bird species are found in northwestern metropolitan areas, but five species are memorable and easy to spot. Three are small but fascinating birds that might visit just about any back yard. Two are spectacular birds of prey that thrive in urban landscapes because of their affinity for nesting on man-made structures and their taste for pigeons, rats, and other animals associated with humans. Whether it is a dainty backyard visitor, a chimney-filling flock, or a downtown pigeon predator, each bird adds an essential dimension to city life.

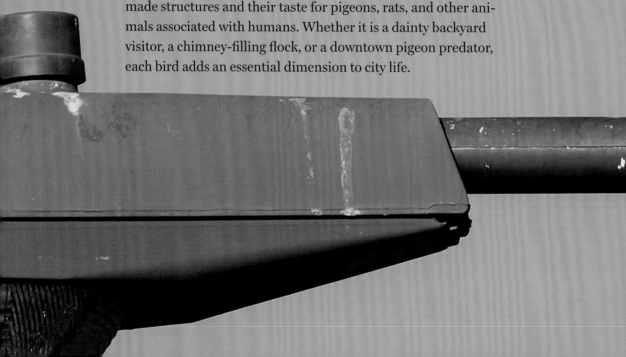

Red-Tailed Hawk

RED-TAILED HAWK
Buteo jamaicensis

Juvenile
Red-tailed
Hawk

DON'T TAKE Red-tailed Hawks for granted just because they are more abundant than gas stations as you drive along the highway. These beautiful birds have carved out a niche among our roads, houses, and skyscrapers, asking only for a steady supply of rodents and pigeons. You might get to watch one soar in a sunny sky, showing off its namesake red tail, or dive from a lamppost onto an unsuspecting vole in a grassy right-of-way. Any chance to observe a bird of prey going about its daily life is a privilege and a delight.

An upright, brown, football-sized raptor perched near an open area can quickly be identified as a hawk. Red-tails are the most commonly seen hawks in the Northwest, but you can check their field marks to be certain. They come in a dizzying variety of plumages, but a few markings are almost always present. Look for a dark band of feathers across the belly,

small white streaks on the shoulders when perched, and a dark leading edge of the wing when you're viewing one from below. You'll see a reddish tail on most adults, but note that juveniles have brown tails.

FOOD AND FORAGING

Red-tails use their sharp talons to capture a diverse array of animal prey, which they pick apart with their hooked bill, eventually swallowing the entire animal—meat, bones, fur, and all. Like owls, they regurgitate indigestible parts in a pellet. Red-tails are a friend both to farmer and urban-dweller because they often eat nuisance animals such as rats and pigeons.

PAIRING AND PARENTING

This bird is a generalist in its nest site selection, nesting in whatever nature, or man, has to offer. Famous pairs of Red-tails have nested on a fire escape in downtown Portland and on an apartment balcony above New York's Central Park. Nesting birds thrive in cities, sometimes producing more young per year than their rural counterparts. Adults line their nests with greenery before laying two or three eggs. Parents share incubation duties during a 28-day period. They hunt birds, mammals, and reptiles and bring them to the nest, feeding little pieces to the young while they are small. Larger nestlings are able to pick apart delivered prey at their leisure. The young hawks leave their nest after 40 days, but they stay close to their parents for at least ten weeks.

MIGRATIONS AND MOVEMENTS

You'll see Red-tails year-round in the Pacific Northwest, especially west of the Cascades, where winters are mild. City-dwelling birds begin nesting in late winter or early spring, and young may leave the nest before the start of summer. Adults leave high-elevation breeding areas during winter, and many dwell in urban areas before returning to nesting sites in late March.

WHERE TO FIND RED-TAILED HAWKS

Finding a Red-tailed Hawk is often as simple as driving down a road through open country. They are the most common and widely distributed birds of prey in the area, and the first hawk you see will likely be a Red-tail. Check perches such as power poles, streetlights, and billboards, and look up for soaring birds. Listen for their famous screech, a mainstay of Western movie sound effects. The abundance and widespread distribution of this species in the Pacific Northwest makes it unnecessary to list specific sites.

OTHER BIRDS TO SEE

The Red-tailed Hawk is just one of a number of species that you can identify from a car travelling at highway speeds (while someone else drives, of course). Also watch for BALD EAGLES, American Kestrels, GREAT BLUE HERONS, Great Egrets, COMMON RAVENS, and Western Scrub-Jays.

VAUX'S SWIFT

Chaetura vauxi

Vaux's Swifts approach a chimney roost at dusk

AS SUNSET APPROACHES on a cool September night, a huge crowd of adults and kids settles in on blankets and lawn chairs waiting for the show. Fireworks? No. Swifts. Who would have thought that a small gray bird could draw such crowds? The magic of Vaux's Swifts is in the way that they form twittering flocks of thousands that spiral into the shapes of discs and tornados before pouring into a chimney in the fading light. Adding to the spectacle are the birds of prey that attend the event to take advantage of the fluttering buffet. The nightly performances of migrating Vaux's Swifts are truly wonders of the urban world.

With their long, curved wings and stubby tails, Vaux's Swifts are shaped like flying cigars. They appear black when you view them against the sky, but they are actually a nondescript gray. If you see a patch of white or another color on a bird, you are not looking at a Vaux's Swift. Swifts are always flying when you see them, and they flutter their wings rapidly without pulling them in close to their body. Swallows forage on the wing like swifts, but with practice, birders can distinguish a swallow's swooping and gliding flight patterns from the stiff-winged flitting of a swift. Swallows will also perch on a power line or a branch, but a Vaux's Swift never will.

FOOD AND FORAGING

When not roosting at night or sitting on a nest, Vaux's Swifts are flying and flying, catching insects and other airborne arthropods. Foraging flights take place at a variety of heights over forests, water, cities, and open fields. Swifts capture food in their beak and store boluses (balls) of arthropods in their mouth when gathering food for nestlings.

PAIRING AND PARENTING

Vaux's Swifts historically nested inside hollow trees of old-growth forests, but they have adapted to urban areas by nesting in chimneys. In forests, they nest inside trees that have been hollowed out by decay. In some cases, they use holes created by roosting Pileated Woodpeckers to enter the tree. Pairs build a small nest cup by snapping twigs off plants and bringing them inside. They have specialized saliva that they use to glue nest material into a half-moon–shaped nest cup that is attached to the interior wall of the tree or chimney. Both parents incubate six or seven eggs for 18 days, brood the nestlings, and feed them thousands of insects a day. Twenty days after hatching, nestlings crawl out of the nest and cling to the wall of the nest cavity with their feet. About a week later, they can fly nearly as well as their parents.

MIGRATIONS AND MOVEMENTS

Northwest populations of Vaux's Swifts are migratory and fly south following their breeding season. Most spend the winter in Mexico, Central America, or Venezuela, but a few sometimes winter in the southern United States. They return to the Northwest in April and nest during the spring and summer months. Large, spectacular flocks gather at nighttime roosts in Oregon and Washington prior to departing the region in the fall.

WHERE TO FIND VAUX'S SWIFTS

During the day, Vaux's Swifts fly high in the sky over cities, forests, and wetlands looking for flying insects. September is the best time to watch the hypnotic spectacle of thousands descending into a chimney at sunset, although some might still be present in October.

In Washington

Frank Wagner Elementary School in Monroe

The Old School House in Selleck, east of Maple Valley

In Oregon

Chapman Elementary School in Portland

University of Oregon's Agate Hall in Eugene

Oregon City High School in Oregon City

OTHER BIRDS TO SEE

Predators such as Cooper's Hawks and PER-
EGRINE FALCONS can put on quite a show as
they try to catch Vaux's Swifts attempting to
enter or leave a chimney.

ANNA'S HUMMINGBIRD

Calypte anna

Male Anna's Hummingbird

ANNA'S HUMMINGBIRDS ARE not only strikingly beautiful and delicate, but they are also tough as nails. They are the only hummingbirds that stay in the Pacific Northwest all year, and their nesting season begins in winter, with the female sometimes getting snowed on while she incubates. This single mom will even defend her nest against predators such as jays and hawks. This would be akin to a human mother fighting off an orca or a polar bear with a small, pointed stick. Pretty impressive for a bird that weighs less than two pennies.

Both males and females have slim green bodies with light bellies. Males have an iridescent fuchsia helmet, and females have a small spot of the same color on their throat. Rufous Hummingbirds are smaller and are a rusty color all over (males) or on their flanks (females).

FOOD AND FORAGING

This species uses its long bill and tongue to collect nectar from flowers and hummingbird feeders. The historic range of the Anna's was confined to areas where flowering plants were available in winter, such as Southern California and Arizona. Thanks to the landscaping and bird feeding that has accompanied the urbanization of the Pacific Northwest, Anna's can find year-round food as far north as Vancouver Island, British Columbia, so they stay throughout the winter. Insects are also available year-round and form a major portion of adult and nestling diets. Adults catch insects by gleaning them from vegetation and capturing them in flight.

PAIRING AND PARENTING

Throughout their range, Anna's Hummingbirds nest earlier in the year than other hummingbird species. Like other hummingbirds, males mate with multiple females and do not provide parental care. Females select nest sites based on proximity to a nectar source. The nest is constructed of plant materials and held together with collected spiderwebs. The female incubates two eggs for about 16 days and feeds the jellybean-sized nestlings regurgitated insects and nectar.

A female Anna's Hummingbird feeds a nestling.

MIGRATIONS AND MOVEMENTS

In urban and coastal areas, where flowering plants, insects, and feeders are present, you can see Anna's throughout the year. Females begin nesting in late January or early February and will continue into the middle of summer. In urban areas with plenty of food, males vigorously defend their feeding or breeding territories throughout the year.

WHERE TO FIND ANNA'S HUMMINGBIRDS

Hummingbird feeders and flower-filled gardens are the best places to find Anna's Hummingbirds. They can be very territorial; once you find them, you can check in on them often.

If you decide to feed hummingbirds, always make a solution of real sugar and water in a ratio of 1 part sugar to 4 parts water, and clean the feeder regularly. Despite the Anna's flashy colors, you might hear one before you see it. Territorial males sing high-pitched songs and produce a loud squeak with their tail feathers during their diving display.

OTHER BIRDS TO SEE

In a garden with well-stocked feeders and inviting trees and shrubs, you can also find BLACK-HEADED GROSBEAKS, American Goldfinches, House Finches, RED-BREASTED NUTHATCHES, BUSHTITS, Black-capped Chickadees, Downy Woodpeckers, and Dark-eyed Juncos.

PEREGRINE FALCON

Falco peregrinus

PEREGRINE FALCONS ARE speed and power manifested in avian form, and they were almost lost to us forever. The insidious effects of the pesticide DDT on the eggs of falcons and other raptors decimated their populations, and by 1970 Peregrines were extremely rare and none were found nesting in the state of Oregon. The banning of DDT and subsequent captive breeding and release programs slowly increased the number of wild Peregrines, and they began expanding into new areas. Portland and the cities throughout the Puget Trough offer infrastructure for nesting that mimics the Peregrine's preferred cliffs as well as an abundance of tasty pigeons and starlings. The urban Peregrines have been prolific: Portland's Fremont Bridge celebrated its fiftieth fledgling in 2010.

Falcons can be identified in flight by their pointed, rapidly flapping wings. Adult Peregrines can be distinguished from other falcons by their dark head and facial feathers that resemble a helmet and their contrasting white neck and breast. Adults also display dark barring on their lower breast and a slate-gray back. Juveniles have brown streaks on their breast and a brown back.

FOOD AND FORAGING

These bird-hunting specialists also capture mammals and insects. No bird is too small and few are too large to be hunted. Peregrines use a number of aerial maneuvers, such as spectacular steep dives, or stoops, at speeds greater than 200 mph, to catch flying birds or knock them to the ground. Once prey is caught, the Peregrine uses its notched bill to sever the spine of its prey, even if the animal is already dead. Males tend to hunt smaller prey, such as songbirds and shorebirds, while females pursue larger birds, such as waterfowl and seabirds.

PAIRING AND PARENTING

Like other falcons, Peregrines do not gather material to build a nest. They use whatever space they can find high on a tall structure such as a cliff, bridge, or skyscraper and lay a clutch of three to five eggs on a bare surface. Breeding pairs begin their conspicuous courtship activities as early as the fall, but they won't lay eggs for months. Both parents incubate the eggs during a 33-day period. Young are capable of making their first perilous flights after 40 days in the nest, and 20 days later, they can fly as well as their parents.

MIGRATIONS AND MOVEMENTS

Peregrine Falcons are known for their long migrations, or peregrinations—hence their name. During migrations and post-breeding dispersals, you might spot them flying over just about any habitat type. Many spend their winters on the Oregon and Washington coasts and in lowland areas after breeding farther to the north. Individuals that breed in low-elevation areas of the Northwest nest in the spring and summer, but they remain in their nesting territories year-round.

WHERE TO FIND PEREGRINE FALCONS

If you visit a nest site during the nesting season (March through June), you may see parents bringing food to the nest and defending the area from any creature that gets too close. Check perches near nest sites such as lampposts and bridge arches. If you see a flock of pigeons flying rapidly, look to see if the birds are being pursued. Audubon Society of Portland offers a Peregrine Watch program on Saturday afternoons in May and June, where volunteers are on hand with spotting scopes to help you see the Marquam Bridge nest.

In Washington

Washington Mutual Building in Seattle

Ship Canal Bridge, Ballard Bridge, and West Seattle Bridge in Seattle

Murray Morgan Bridge in Tacoma

Port of Olympia crane

In Oregon

Cape Meares State Park near Tillamook

Marquam Bridge, Saint Johns Bridge, and Fremont Bridge in Portland

The Glen L. Jackson Bridge, Interstate 205, that spans the Columbia River between Oregon and Washington

OTHER BIRDS TO SEE

As you are standing near water, scanning the sky, look for Double-crested Cormorants, BALD EAGLES, RED-TAILED HAWKS, Canada Geese, and GREAT BLUE HERONS.

BUSHTIT

Psaltriparus minimus

FOOD AND FORAGING

While hanging upside down or briefly hovering, these featherlight birds scour the branch tips of shrubs and trees for invertebrates to pluck with their tiny bills. Foraging flocks can fill trees and shrubs with as many as 50 individuals and make quite a sight when they cover every square inch of a suet feeder during a Bushtit free-for-all.

PAIRING AND PARENTING

In late winter, pairs start to form within flocks. Each pair breaks away from the flock and works together to create an intricate hanging nest with an entrance near the top, where it is attached to a branch. Nests are often built in drooping branches of large trees, but small shrubs are used as well. The nest is usually placed in an area that receives direct sunlight to warm the four to eight eggs while adults are off the nest and foraging. Parents alternate incubation duties for 13 days. Nestlings are fed by both parents and occasionally by helpers, which can be siblings that fledged from an earlier nest, adults that failed to find a mate, or pairs whose previous nest attempt failed. Young leave the nest 18 days after hatching.

THE BUSHTIT IS a small bird that makes a big impression. These tiny, acrobatic puffballs are a great source of entertainment at the bird feeder when they arrive in hordes and cling to each other's tails to try to get their turn at the suet. In the winter they fill the trees with high-pitched chatter, and in the spring they build big stretchy nests that hang from the trees like tube socks made of lichen. The best thing about Bushtits is that you'll often find them right in your own back yard.

Bushtits are very small and uniformly gray with round heads, short necks, and long tails. Much of their 4½ inches of length consists of tail, and the rest is mostly puffy feathers. Adult males and females can be differentiated by the male's dark eyes and the female's pale eyes.

Male
Bushtit

MIGRATIONS AND MOVEMENTS

Bushtits are not migratory, but flocks make seasonal movements to find food or escape harsh weather. Pairs will begin nest construction in March if the weather is mild. Otherwise, they put off nest-building until April or May. At the end of the breeding season, flocks reconvene until the next spring.

WHERE TO FIND BUSHTITS

If you live in the city, you do not need to travel far to find a Bushtit flock or a nest. They will forage in native and nonnative trees or shrubs,

Bushtit nest

so a well-landscaped back yard or city park can be a great place to start. Pairs will nest just about anywhere with trees, but parks with healthy wetlands and native plants tend to have the greatest densities of nests. At any time of the year, listen for the high-pitched "pish, pish" calls of pairs or flocks, and scan trees and shrubs for movement. Keep an eye on suet feeders that attract hungry flocks. From March to June, scan the branches for their large, hanging nests. If the nest is still in use, it won't be long before the parents appear.

In Washington

Green Lake Park in Seattle

Magnuson Park in Seattle

Kent Ponds in the Green River Natural
    Resources Area near Seattle

China Lake Park in Tacoma

In Oregon

Oaks Bottom Wildlife Refuge in Portland

Alton Baker Park in Eugene

Minto-Brown Island Park in Salem

Mount Tabor Park in Portland

OTHER BIRDS TO SEE

Bushtits are not the only species with nests that are easy to observe in city parks. American Robins and ANNA'S HUMMINGBIRDS also nest in shrubs or in the lower branches of trees. Northern Flickers, Downy Woodpeckers, Black-capped Chickadees, and RED-BREASTED SAPSUCKERS nest in the cavities of snags or dead branches of live trees. If you are lucky, you will find the nests of larger birds, such as GREAT-HORNED OWLS, RED-TAILED HAWKS, and GREAT BLUE HERONS, near the tops of large trees.

WEEKEND BIRDING TRIPS

Morning in the Klamath Basin, Oregon

San Juan Islands
Mt. Baker
Vancouver Island
① Skagit Valley
● MOUNT VERNON
Salish Sea
WASHINGTON
PORT TOWNSEND ②
● EVERETT
Olympic Mountains
● SEATTLE
④
Puget Sound
PACIFIC
● TACOMA
Mt. Rainier
⑤
OLYMPIA
● YAKIMA
Grays Harbor
Mt. Adams
Willapa Bay
Mt. St. Helens
Columbia River
CANNON BEACH ●
Coast Range
Mt. Hood
Tillamook Bay
③
● PORTLAND
Willamette River
Mt. Jefferson
NEWPORT ●
● SALEM
Yaquina Bay
⑥
● CORVALLIS
OCEAN
⑦
● BEND
EUGENE ●
OREGON
COOS BAY ●
Cascade
Siskiyou Mountains
● MEDFORD
⑧
● ASHLAND
● KLAMATH FALLS

Eight Birding Weekends

WINTER WEEKENDS, NORTH TO SOUTH

Washington Park near Anacortes, Washington

① VALLEY OF THE SWANS

SKAGIT AND ISLAND COUNTIES, WASHINGTON, IN WINTER

Trumpeter
Swans

Mount Vernon

Mount Vernon, Washington, is located in the middle of excellent birding sites and is just the right size to explore on foot during non-birding times of day. Local businesses love visiting birders, and hotels offer maps of the best local birding sites.

BEST TIME OF YEAR:

November through February

The highest concentrations of raptors and waterfowl are found during the winter months. Come spring, the area is overrun with tulip enthusiasts.

FAMOUS FOR GIANT Trumpeter Swans, clouds of Snow Geese, and large wintertime gatherings of Bald Eagles, the Skagit Valley offers these birds and more to hardy winter birders. Skagit and Island Counties include unique habitats where farm fields meet bays and salt marshes, providing small mammals, eelgrass, and fish for a dizzying number of wintering birds of prey. Far enough north to attract Gyrfalcons and Snowy Owls, the area hosts these rarities more often than other places in the Pacific Northwest. An abundance of public land with access for birders (and hunters) lets you get out of your car and explore, and fields dotted with antique farmhouses and barns make for a beautiful backdrop.

PLACES TO GO

Padilla Bay

Padilla Bay is home to a rare eelgrass habitat that attracts scores of Brant and other waterfowl every winter. Bayview State Park and the nearby Breazeale Padilla Bay Interpretive Center offer views of the bay. The interpretive center is great for birders of all abilities and offers bird checklists, displays, and aquaria filled with local sea life. MUST-SEE BIRDS: Common Loons, Great Blue Herons, Brant, and Eurasian Wigeons. OTHER INTERESTING BIRDS: Northern Pintails and other waterfowl.

Samish Flats and Samish Island

The Samish Flats area, or the West 90, is well known in local birding circles for its abundance of Short-eared Owls. The area's fields and brush are also excellent places to see other raptors, including a falcon grand slam of Peregrine Falcons, American Kestrels, Prairie Falcons, Merlins, and Gyrfalcons. Just to the north, a small county park on a cliff on Samish Island is the best place in the area to view seabirds. MUST-SEE BIRDS: Bald Eagles, Short-eared Owls, Red-breasted Mergansers, Surf Scoters, Northern Shrikes, and Common Ravens. OTHER INTERESTING BIRDS: Rough-legged Hawks, Common Goldeneyes, and a variety of seabirds.

Fir Island and Skagit Wildlife Area

You wouldn't necessarily know that you are on an island, but this area is delineated by the north and south forks of the Skagit River. The many access points to the wildlife area offer views of dikes, fields, bays, and tidal creeks. If one point seems too quiet, just drive down the road a mile to the next one. MUST-SEE BIRDS: Western Meadowlarks, Bald Eagles, Northern Harriers, Short-eared Owls, Trumpeter Swans, and Northern Shrikes. OTHER INTERESTING BIRDS: Snow Geese and Marsh Wrens.

Eide Road near Stanwood

This area is out of the way but worth seeking out. If you take the path beside the bramble-covered dike, you can scan the fields and shrubs at the same time. Walk one of several pathways to climb up the dike for views of the Still-aguamish River and Port Susan. MUST-SEE BIRDS: Western Meadowlarks, Northern Harriers, Short-eared Owls, Great Blue Herons, and Belted Kingfishers. OTHER INTERESTING BIRDS: Rough-legged Hawks and Snowy Owls (in some years).

Butler Flats near Burlington

Separated from the other birding sites by Interstate 5, the Butler Flats area offers more farm fields and utility poles to scan for the area's specialties. MUST-SEE BIRDS: Bald Eagles and Trumpeter Swans. OTHER INTERESTING BIRDS: Tundra Swans, Gyrfalcons (rare), and American Kestrels.

TIPS FOR BIRDING IN SKAGIT AND ISLAND COUNTIES

- Drive the small roads that crisscross the area to find interesting raptors in fields and perched on utility poles.
- Respect private property and uphold the good reputation that birders strive to keep.
- If you don't want to hear gunshots as you bird, wait until late January, after hunting season ends.
- Winter is low season for hotel rates, so look for midweek hotel deals that leave you some extra cash for hot coffee and Snow Goose souvenirs.
- Washington's Discover Pass is required at many parks, and you can purchase an annual pass ahead of time online or at a sporting goods store. It is well worth the money not to have to deal with a day use fee. Don't try to avoid buying a pass if you want to visit an area that requires one: the fines are hefty if you get a ticket. Just keep the pass hanging from your rearview mirror.

SHELTER FROM THE STORM

THE SALISH SEA IN WINTER

Port Townsend's boat basin

A pair
of Surf
Scoters

THE SALISH SEA'S huge expanse of protected water is a wintertime refuge for seagoing murrelets, auklets, and ducks. Around every corner is a bay, channel, or passage likely to be visited by some sort of interesting water bird. The Strait of San Juan de Fuca is a major passageway for seabirds seeking refuge from rough winter waves. These birds, often inaccessible at sea or nesting far to the north, are easily viewed from numerous public access sites. Many of the birding sites in this area host similar collections of species, but you might need to try several spots to find all the birds you are looking for.

PLACES TO GO, FROM EAST TO WEST

Fort Flagler State Park near Port Townsend
This state park offers many places to view birds on the water. The east side looks over the large Admiralty Inlet, and the west side faces the smaller Kilisut Harbor. As you drive through the park, each fork in the road takes you to a different vantage point and habitat. MUST-SEE BIRDS: Bald Eagles, Peregrine Falcons, Common Murres, Harlequin Ducks, Brant, Great Blue Herons, and Black Oystercatchers. OTHER INTERESTING BIRDS: Ancient Murrelets, Black Scoters, and Red-throated Loons.

Fort Worden State Park near Port Townsend

With its large campground, sandy beach, and requisite lighthouse, this park's biggest attraction from a birding point of view is Point Wilson, which goes right out into the straight with lots of birds to see on both sides. MUST-SEE BIRDS: Common Loons, Harlequin Ducks, Common Murres, and Pigeon Guillemots. OTHER INTERESTING BIRDS: Ancient Murrelets, Red-necked Grebes, White-winged Scoters, and Mew Gulls.

Marlyn Nelson County Park at Port Williams

Protected waters at the mouth of Sequim Bay afford you close views of seabirds as they feed, preen, and relax away from the straight's massive swells. MUST-SEE BIRDS: Marbled Murrelets, Pigeon Guillemots, Red-breasted Mergansers, Long-tailed Ducks, and Harlequin Ducks. OTHER INTERESTING BIRDS: Common Goldeneyes and Pacific Loons.

Dungeness National Wildlife Refuge near Sequim

This refuge gives you access to the long, hike-able Graveyard Spit, with the Straight of San Juan de Fuca on one side and the protected Dungeness Bay on the other. Even if you don't make it the 5 miles to the lighthouse, you'll enjoy some amazing views and see some great birds. MUST-SEE BIRDS: Bald Eagles, Peregrine Falcons, Northern Harriers, Brant, Marbled Murrelets, Eurasian Wigeons, and Long-tailed Ducks. OTHER INTERESTING BIRDS: Pacific Loons and Northern Pintails. The occasional stray Snowy Owl spends the winter here.

Bonus: Keystone Ferry from Port Townsend to Whidbey Island

If you can fit it into your schedule, this 30-minute ferry jaunt is a great opportunity to look for seabirds out on the open water. Crockett Lake is right across the street from the ferry landing on Whidbey Island, and it hosts a plethora of wintering ducks. MUST-SEE BIRDS: Marbled Murrelets, Surf Scoters, Ruddy Ducks, and Common Murres. OTHER INTERESTING BIRDS: Ancient Murrelets, Pelagic Cormorants, Black-bellied Plovers, Horned Grebes, and White-winged Scoters.

TIPS FOR BIRDING THE SALISH SEA

- When you are birding mostly on the water, glare can be a major factor. Try to choose your birding times and sites so that the sun is behind you, lighting up the birds you want to see.
- Tidal rips are choppy areas of strong-moving current that occur off points of land as the tide changes. They are full of fish and krill and attract large numbers of feeding seabirds.
- Buy or borrow a spotting scope for this trip. Many birds are far enough away to be barely identifiable with binoculars, and a scope gives you a chance to appreciate their plumage and behavior.
- Winter is low season for hotel rates, so look for midweek hotel deals that leave you some extra cash for hot coffee and ferry tickets.
- Washington's Discover Pass is required at many parks, and you can purchase an annual pass ahead of time online or at a sporting goods store. It is well worth the money not to have to deal with a day use fee. Don't try to avoid buying a pass if you want to visit an area that requires one: the fines are hefty if you get a ticket. Just keep the pass hanging from your rearview mirror.

3

GRAY SKIES AND GREAT BIRDS

THE NORTHERN OREGON COAST IN WINTER

Male
Harlequin
Ducks

Manzanita and Cannon Beach

Manzanita and Cannon Beach are located near excellent birding sites and are delightful towns in their own right.

BEST TIME OF YEAR:

December through April

Birding the Oregon Coast is rewarding year-round, but winter and early spring months offer empty beaches and a great diversity and abundance of seabirds and waterfowl.

EACH FALL, great numbers of birds converge from breeding sites in Alaska, arctic Canada, and inland lakes to fill the comparatively temperate bays, coves, and sewage lagoons of the Oregon Coast. Everywhere you turn, you can see loons, grebes, ducks, geese, and enough gulls to keep even the more experienced birders reaching for the field guide. Some people will tell you that winter at the Oregon Coast is miserably wet and cold, but think how uncrowded the beaches are with all those people staying home. Anyway, there is always the satisfaction of tallying up the day's bird list over a bowl of clam chowder or a pint of dark beer while the storm rages outside.

PLACES TO GO, FROM NORTH TO SOUTH

Cannon Beach Settling Ponds

These ponds near downtown Cannon Beach host a variety of ducks and the occasional seabird blown in from the ocean. MUST-SEE BIRDS: Bald Eagles and Wood Ducks. OTHER INTERESTING BIRDS: Marsh Wrens, Buffleheads, and dabbling and diving ducks.

Haystack Rock in Cannon Beach

Visit Haystack Rock at low tide to get close looks at birds on and around the rock. MUST-SEE BIRDS: Black Turnstones, Harlequin Ducks, Black Oystercatchers, Surf Scoters, and Brant. OTHER INTERESTING BIRDS: Pelagic Cormorants and White-winged Scoters. The famous Tufted Puffins arrive in April.

Nehalem Bay Sewage Ponds in Nehalem

The odor can be a little off-putting, but the birds you'll see are worth it. On the way to the ponds, you'll pass through meadows that are filled with raptors. Be sure to follow the posted regulations at the ponds: as you enter the pedestrian gate, only the path on your right is open to visitors. MUST-SEE BIRDS: White-tailed Kites, Northern Harriers, and Bald Eagles in the meadows; Wood Ducks and Ruddy Ducks in the ponds. OTHER INTERESTING BIRDS: Northern Shovelers, Greater Scaups, Buffleheads, Gadwalls, and Ring-necked Ducks.

Barview Jetty

Always use good judgment around jetties. Waves can crash over the top without warning. Scan the mouth of Tillamook Bay and the ocean north of it from the jetty for birds. MUST-SEE BIRDS: Pigeon Guillemots, Surf Scoters, Common Loons, Western Grebes, and Black Turnstones. OTHER INTERESTING BIRDS: Pacific Loons, Surfbirds, White-winged Scoters, and Black Scoters.

Three Graces Tidal Area near Barview

This extremely photogenic site off Highway 101 offers plenty of rocks for perching seabirds and deep channels for diving birds. Take the path just across the railroad tracks. MUST-SEE BIRDS: Common Loons, Surf Scoters, Pigeon Guillemots, Brandt's Cormorants, and Black Oystercatchers. OTHER INTERESTING BIRDS: Pelagic Cormorants and Red-throated Loons.

Pacific Oyster Company store and restaurant in Bay City

If you like seafood, stop in for some oysters to show your appreciation for public access to this great birding spot. A nearby muddy inlet is perfect for shorebirds, and you'll enjoy expansive views of Tillamook Bay. This is the most reliable place in the area to see Black Turnstones; check the abandoned boat and the rocky areas on both sides of the point. MUST-SEE BIRDS: Western Grebes and Belted Kingfishers. OTHER INTERESTING BIRDS: Common Goldeneyes, American Wigeons, and Horned Grebes.

Bayocean Spit

With Tillamook Bay to the east and Cape Meares Lake to the west, the access roads on the Bayocean Spit offer great birding opportunities. From the parking lot, you can hike along an old road to catch more glimpses of the bay and its birds. MUST SEE BIRDS: Belted Kingfishers, Bald Eagles, Great Blue Herons, Eurasian Wigeons, and Brant. OTHER INTERESTING BIRDS: Greater Scaups, Pintails, and Ring-necked Ducks.

Cape Meares State Park

Follow the Three Capes Scenic Drive, which goes from Pacific City to Tillamook, to reach this promontory that provides great views of the ocean. Hike the quarter mile to the lighthouse to scan the ocean for interesting seabirds. You can enjoy views of a protected cove from an observation deck adjacent to the parking lot. A preserved forest harbors songbirds and giant mossy trees, including a famous misshapen Sitka spruce called the Octopus Tree. MUST-SEE BIRDS: Brown Creepers, Varied Thrushes, Peregrine Falcons, Marbled Murrelets, Pigeon Guillemots, and Surf Scoters. OTHER INTERESTING BIRDS: Golden-crowned Kinglets, Pacific Loons, and Red-necked Grebes.

Netarts Bay

Head south along Netarts Bay Drive in Netarts as it closely follows the bay. Several pullouts offer safe places to pull over and view waterfowl. MUST-SEE BIRDS: Harlequin Ducks, Surf Scoters, Red-breasted Mergansers, Western Grebes, Common Loons, Great Blue Herons, Bald Eagles, and Peregrine Falcons. OTHER INTERESTING BIRDS: Common Goldeneyes and Red-necked Grebes.

TIPS FOR BIRDING THE NORTHERN OREGON COAST

- Often the rainy weather comes in waves, and you can squeeze in some birding between storms.
- Respect the power of the ocean. All those signs warning you about sneaker waves and car-sized floating logs are there for a reason.
- Be wary around jetties, especially during stormy conditions.
- Invest in good raingear (including pants).
- A decent spotting scope will allow you to get much more satisfying looks at seabirds and waterfowl than a great pair of binoculars.
- Bring a soft cotton cloth to wipe raindrops from the lens of your scope or binoculars.

SPRING AND SUMMER WEEKENDS, NORTH TO SOUTH

Smith Rock State Park near Redmond, Oregon

④
URBAN BIRDIN'
SPRINGTIME IN PUGET SOUND

An Osprey visits
its nest.

Seattle

Seattle is known for its natural beauty, with water all around and snow-capped vistas in every direction. In every part of the city, parks and natural areas are worthy of a visit; deciding which ones to visit in a weekend might be the most difficult part. And with more restaurants and brewpubs than you could visit in a year, Seattle is practically irresistible.

BEST TIME OF YEAR:

May and June

During migration time in May, large numbers of colorful and singing birds move through the Seattle area, and you'll find them easily. The business of nest building and nestling feeding follows, with busy birds drawing lots of attention. By late June, much of the action has slowed and some birds, especially migrants, can be more difficult to find.

ALTHOUGH THE WATERS of Puget Sound are at their birdiest in the winter, an influx of colorful migrant land birds spices things up each spring and makes birding in this area a delight. Seattle's official bird, the Great Blue Heron, is abundant in the local waters, joined by its smaller, more secretive cousin, the Green Heron. Aim your binoculars a little higher into the trees and shrubs to find tanagers, grosbeaks, crossbills, and woodpeckers to add to your list.

PLACES TO GO

Lake Sammamish State Park near Issaquah

Follow the trails through the forest and among wooded ponds and creeks to find forest specialists such as Red-breasted Sapsuckers and shy wetland dwellers such as Green Herons. Walk the long stretch of beach along Lake Sammamish, and you'll spot lots of birds in this large, popular park. MUST-SEE BIRDS: Bald Eagles, Green Herons, Wood Ducks, Band-tailed Pigeons, Red-breasted Sapsuckers, Black-headed Grosbeaks, and Belted Kingfishers. OTHER INTERESTING BIRDS: Bullock's Orioles, Chestnut-backed Chickadees, Common Mergansers, and American Goldfinches.

Magnuson Park in Seattle

Located on the western shore of Lake Washington, this large park combines lakeshore, forest patches, and wetlands. The wetlands are the highlight of the park and are surrounded by native vegetation and walking trails. Winter offers more water birds on the lake, but during the summer, check the swimming platform for terns and gulls. MUST-SEE BIRDS: California Quail, Anna's Hummingbirds, and Caspian Terns. OTHER INTERESTING BIRDS: Spotted Sandpipers, Gadwalls, and White-crowned Sparrows.

Union Bay Natural Area near Lake Washington

From a former landfill has sprung a bird magnet of a natural area that is always worth a visit. Where the covered landfill settled unevenly, lily pad–laden ponds and marshes are filled with ducks and rails. Willows and larger trees provide perches and nesting sites for other birds. MUST-SEE BIRDS: Cinnamon Teals, Great Blue Herons, Western Kingbirds, Hooded Mergansers, and Vaux's Swifts. OTHER INTERESTING BIRDS: Pied-billed Grebes, Common Yellowthroats, and Virginia Rails.

Discovery Park in Magnolia

It's difficult to describe the terrain of this huge park, because it varies from coniferous and deciduous forest, to open fields, to the waters of Puget Sound. If you hike all the way out to the point, you may catch a glimpse of a passing seabird. MUST-SEE BIRDS: Pileated Woodpeckers, Western Tanagers, Red Crossbills, Olive-sided Flycatchers, and Evening Grosbeaks. OTHER INTERESTING BIRDS: Black-throated Gray Warblers, Golden-crowned Kinglets, and Northern Rough-winged Swallows.

NORTH TO EVERETT

Drive a few minutes north of Seattle, and you can visit several birding sites that are special enough to warrant a side trip.

Spencer Island Park and the Everett Sewage Ponds

Ownership of Spencer Island is split between Snohomish County and the Washington Department of Wildlife. Both halves of the park, and the gravel road that leads into it from the parking area, are great places to spot birds. You can walk a series of trails and dikes to explore the tidally influenced sloughs and wetlands. The nearby Everett Sewage Ponds can be scoped from the road outside the gates, or you can apply at the plant office for a free permit to enter and walk the perimeter. At the ponds, you might find an interesting selection of ducks and gulls at any time of year. MUST-SEE BIRDS: Cinnamon Teals, Northern Harriers, Violet-green Swallows, and Western Tanagers. OTHER INTERESTING BIRDS: Blue-winged Teals, Willow Flycatchers, Yellow Warblers, Downy Woodpeckers, and Marsh Wrens.

Port Gardner

The pilings in Port Gardner are home to an unusually large nesting colony of Ospreys. Visit here in the summer to see them flying by, sitting on nests, eating fish, and calling to one another. Check the nearby mudflats for shorebirds and waterfowl. MUST-SEE BIRDS: Ospreys, Great Blue Herons, and Whimbrels. OTHER INTERESTING BIRDS: Purple Martins, American Wigeons, and Gadwalls.

TIPS FOR BIRDING PUGET SOUND

- Washington's Discover Pass is required at many state parks, including Lake Sammamish State Park. You can buy an annual pass ahead of time online or at a sporting goods store. It is well worth the money not to have to deal with a day use fee. Don't try to avoid buying a pass if you want to visit an area that requires one: the fines are hefty if you get a ticket. Just keep the pass hanging from your rearview mirror.
- Parking is hard to come by near the Union Bay Natural Area because it's near the University of Washington campus. If you visit after the start of summer vacation in early June, parking may be easier to find.
- Peregrine Falcons often nest on local bridges. Contact Seattle Audubon for current information.

BIRDING AMONG THE WINERIES AND ORCHARDS

THE CANYON COUNTRY OF CENTRAL WASHINGTON

Canyon Wren

Yakima

Yakima is centrally located for productive day trips in every direction, and you'll even find a few good birding spots in town. The Cascades lie to the west, Yakima Canyon to the north, sagebrush country and the Columbia River to the east, and wetland refuges to the south. If the afternoons get a little too hot for birding, you can kick back at the nearest winery while the inescapable California Quail call from the vineyard and swallows swoop overhead.

BEST TIME OF YEAR:

May and June

May and June are lively months for birding in Central Washington, with a flurry of color and song. It can get pretty quiet by July, however, when birds have finished defending their territories and the weather heats up.

LEWIS'S WOODPECKERS IN the morning, Canyon Wrens in the afternoon, and Common Nighthawks in the evening make for full, rewarding days of birding. From the forested foothills of the Cascades to the sagebrush-covered canyons, Central Washington includes a great variety of habitats in a small area. When you throw in lush wetlands, you can easily see 100 bird species here in a single weekend.

PLACES TO GO

Yakima Canyon

This scenic route on Highway 821 from Yakima to Ellensburg takes you through steep, rocky cliffs and golden hillsides as you follow the winding path of the Yakima River. Stop at the first few pullouts on the southern end of the road; they are the best for spotting cliff-dwelling birds. MUST-SEE BIRDS: Golden Eagles, Prairie Falcons, Canyon Wrens, Western Kingbirds, and Western Meadowlarks. OTHER INTERESTING BIRDS: White-throated Swifts, American Kestrels, and Bullock's Orioles.

Bethel Ridge Road

Forest Service Road 1500 is a gravel road off Highway 12 that heads up into the mountains. Many species of woodpeckers frequent this area. The road quickly passes through Ponderosa pine forest, wildfire sites, wet meadows, and high-elevation forests, offering a changing community of birds to check out. MUST-SEE BIRDS: Black-backed Woodpeckers (burned trees), Williamson's Sapsuckers (aspen trees), and White-headed Woodpeckers (big pine trees). OTHER INTERESTING BIRDS: Cassin's Finches, Yellow Warblers, and Yellow-rumped Warblers.

Oak Creek Wildlife Area

This hilly area has several access points, but the most interesting place for birding is just west of the elk-feeding area on Highway 12. A gravel road travels through a mixed oak, pine, and cottonwood forest sandwiched between rockier areas. MUST-SEE BIRDS: Canyon Wrens, Lewis's Woodpeckers, American Dippers, Black-headed Grosbeaks, and Western Tanagers. OTHER INTERESTING BIRDS: House Wrens, Red-naped Sapsuckers, and Warbling Vireos.

Wenas Basin

The basin between Yakima and Ellensburg along Wenas Road and Umtanum Road is so dense with birding opportunities that you could spend an entire day exploring it. You'll see trailheads for hikes into dry canyons and along creeks when traveling this route. The rough road along Wenas Creek into the Wenas Campground (the site of the annual Audubon Society gathering) might reward you with White-headed Woodpeckers, Calliope Hummingbirds, Red Crossbills, and an abundance of other birds. Wenas Lake is a great stop for shorebirds in spring and also offers dense riparian vegetation with Yellow-breasted Chats and other songbirds. Umtanum Road is dotted with nest boxes that house Mountain and Western Bluebirds. Along the way, you're likely to see quail, sparrows, woodpeckers, and more.

Yakima Sportsman State Park

This park, just across the river from downtown Yakima, is packed with birds. Small ponds and marshes are loaded with waterfowl and black-birds, and large deciduous trees are filled with many species of songbirds. Interpretive signs along the trail point out the natural features of the park. MUST-SEE BIRDS: Yellow-headed Blackbirds, Cedar Waxwings, Wood Ducks, Black-headed Grosbeaks, and California Quail. OTHER INTERESTING BIRDS: American Gold-finches and Tree Swallows.

Cowiche Canyon Trail

The trail through the canyon is accessible from a trailhead at each end or a connecting trail from the Wilridge Winery (our favorite option). This small canyon offers two birding sites in one with riparian birds in the creekside veg-etation and rock dwellers on the slopes above. MUST-SEE BIRDS: Canyon Wrens, Lazuli Bun-tings, Western Tanagers, Common Nighthawks, and Common Ravens. OTHER INTERESTING BIRDS: Say's Phoebes, Black-billed Magpies, and Rock Wrens.

Toppenish National Wildlife Refuge

This refuge south of Yakima is bordered by sagebrush on one side and irrigated farmland on the other. In between is an oasis of creeks, marshland, and riparian vegetation that is home to an array of birds in every season. An overlook platform gives you great views of the cattail marsh, and the roads that crisscross the refuge put you right in the middle of the action. MUST-SEE BIRDS: American White Pelicans, American Bitterns, Cinnamon Teals, West-ern Meadowlarks, Western Kingbirds, and lots more. OTHER INTERESTING BIRDS: Bank Swallows, Loggerhead Shrikes, Wilson's Snipes, and possibly Blue-winged Teals and Bobolinks.

Fort Simcoe State Park

Located about 40 miles southwest of Yakima, this historic park is filled with oak trees that are home to a large number of Lewis's Woodpeckers.

Bickleton, the Bluebird Capital of the World

The road connecting Goldendale to Bickleton is a great place to see lots of Mountain Bluebirds and a few Western Bluebirds, too. The area around the tiny town of Bickleton is filled with thousands of blue and white birdhouses that attract a huge number of bluebirds each spring.

TIPS FOR BIRDING IN CENTRAL WASHINGTON

- Washington's Discover Pass is required at many parks, and you can buy an annual pass ahead of time online or at a sporting goods store. It is well worth the money not to have to deal with a day use fee. Don't try to avoid buying a pass if you want to visit an area that requires one: the fines are hefty if you get a ticket. Just keep the pass hanging from your rearview mirror.

- As in many places during the summer, you may encounter ticks, especially if you venture off the trail into the brush.

- An extra jug of water is good to have in the car in case you find yourself far from a water source on a hot afternoon.

- A fine-scale map such as a gazetteer is essen-tial for this area, because fold-out maps of the state don't label the roads that connect many of these sites.

- Because many of these sites are not parks, restrooms are few and far between. Gas sta-tions and restaurants are your best bets.

STANDING ROOM ONLY

NESTING SEASON ON THE CENTRAL OREGON COAST

Black
Oystercatcher

IT'S ALWAYS EXCITING to have a front row seat to the nesting behavior of birds. The court-ship displays, feedings, and fuzzy babies create an entertaining spectacle each spring through summer. Although many songbirds hide their nests, seabirds such as murres and cormorants build theirs out in the open and are loud about it, too. Oregon's offshore rocks are protected for the sake of seabirds, and many sites along the coast offer you an elevated view as the birds go about their frenzied business. Summer is also the time to enjoy colorful neotropical migrant songbirds as well as other seasonal visitors such as vultures and terns.

PLACES TO GO, FROM NORTH TO SOUTH

Yaquina Head Outstanding Natural Area in Newport

One of the best places on the Oregon Coast to see (and smell) nesting seabirds, Yaquina Head offers a viewing platform close to offshore nest-ing areas, at just the right height for spying on the birds. A variety of seabirds make their nests in crowded colonies on the nearby rocks and cliffs. Note that an access fee is required to visit this area. Park at the visitor's center and walk the trail to the lighthouse. MUST-SEE BIRDS: Brandt's Cormorants, Common Murres, Pigeon Guillemots, and Black Oystercatchers. Brown Pelicans, Common Ravens, Peregrine Falcons, and Bald Eagles all frequent the area and have been known to eat the young or adult Common Murres.

Hatfield Marine Science Center Trail in Newport

This short, easy trail hugs a section of Yaquina Bay that offers sandbars and shallow feeding areas for birds. Check shrubs and nearby feed-ers on the other side of the trail for interesting songbirds. MUST-SEE BIRDS: Caspian Terns, Whimbrels, and Great Blue Herons. OTHER INTERESTING BIRDS: Purple Martins and White-crowned Sparrows.

Beaver Creek State Natural Area

One of Oregon's newest natural areas, Beaver Creek includes both riparian and upland habi-tats for a great cross-section of species. You can explore it by trail or by canoe. The visitor center has a variety of bird feeders and offers a scenic view of the natural area. MUST-SEE

BIRDS: Watch for Ospreys, Cedar Waxwings, and Band-tailed Pigeons, and listen for the distinctive calls and songs of Swainson's Thrushes, Olive-sided Flycatchers, and Black-headed Grosbeaks. OTHER INTERESTING BIRDS: Turkey Vultures, Cliff Swallows, and Common Yellowthroats.

Seal Rock State Wayside

Offering a great vantage point for floating, feeding, and nesting birds, the Seal Rock Wayside off Highway 101 provides a good view of nearby offshore rocks and intertidal areas. MUST-SEE BIRDS: Brown Pelicans, Black Oystercatchers, Pigeon Guillemots, Brandt's Cormorants, Harlequin Ducks, and Surf Scoters. OTHER INTERESTING BIRDS: Western Gulls and Pelagic Cormorants make their nests on the rocks.

TIPS FOR BIRDING ON THE CENTRAL OREGON COAST

- Summer afternoons on the coast can be very breezy, which makes it difficult to hear and see birds; head out in the mornings for calmer weather.
- Another good reason to bird early is to avoid the distorting, blurring effects caused by rising waves of warm air that can occur as you look through binoculars. You can always pass the afternoon browsing local bookstores and candy shops.

Yaquina Head Outstanding Natural Area in Newport

RED ROCKS, BLUE WATER, AND WHITE-HEADED WOODPECKERS

CENTRAL OREGON IN SUMMER

HEADQUARTERS:

Sisters

Sisters is an adorable western town surrounded on all sides by great birding.

BEST TIME OF YEAR:

May though July

Visit the area during late spring through early summer to see lots of singing and nesting birds.

Male White-headed Wood-pecker

CENTRAL OREGON IS famous for its abundant woodpeckers: 11 species live in the forests around Sisters. Such amazing diversity results from the combination of ancient Ponderosa pines, riparian aspen groves, and wildfire sites that attract tasty beetles. Happily, these habitats, and the drier ones to the east, also make for beautiful scenery you can enjoy as you bird. Seeing the snowy peaks of the Three Sisters and Mount Jefferson glowing against the blue skies of Central Oregon will make you want to stay longer than just a few days.

PLACES TO GO

Calliope Crossing

Located north of Sisters, this area was named for the Calliope Hummingbird, which nests here. Follow the gravel road across the stream, and you end up in the middle of riparian vegetation with great views of notable birds. MUST-SEE BIRDS: Williamson's Sapsuckers, Red-breasted Sapsuckers, Calliope Hummingbirds, Black-headed Grosbeaks, and Western Tanagers. OTHER INTERESTING BIRDS: Northern Goshawks perched in the neighboring pines and Virginia Rails skulking in the water.

Cold Springs and Indian Ford Campgrounds

The combination of dry pine forest and wet areas with aspens make for a great diversity of nesting birds. Cold Springs Campground is located west of Sisters, and Indian Ford is near Black Butte Ranch, northwest of town. MUST-SEE BIRDS: Williamson's Sapsuckers, Red-breasted Sapsuckers, White-headed Woodpeckers, Olive-sided Flycatchers, Green-tailed Towhees, and Red Crossbills. OTHER INTERESTING BIRDS: Chipping Sparrows, Cassin's Finches, and Northern Goshawks. You might also see a variety of Empidonax flycatchers.

Metolius River Trails near Camp Sherman

Downstream of Camp Sherman, trails on both sides follow this dazzling spring-fed river through giant Ponderosa pines. MUST-SEE BIRDS: Ospreys, American Dippers (nesting), White-headed Woodpeckers, Western Tanagers, and Black-headed Grosbeaks. Common Nighthawks are common at dusk. OTHER INTERESTING BIRDS: ubiquitous Yellow Warblers, noisy Pygmy Nuthatches, and families of Common Mergansers.

West Side of Sisters

The bird feeders and pines near the churches, schools, and hotels make this area a magnet for Pinyon Jays.

Burned Areas West and South of Sisters

The desolate appearance of a burned forest is misleading, because these areas are actually full of new plant growth and food for birds. MUST-SEE BIRDS: Black-backed Woodpeckers, Western Bluebirds, and Olive-sided Flycatchers. OTHER INTERESTING BIRDS: Townsend's Solitaires and Three-toed Woodpeckers.

Smith Rock State Park

About 30 minutes northeast of Sisters, this site certainly merits a visit. The Crooked River snakes through tall cliffs, creating a productive gradient of habitats, from dry upland, to riparian. MUST-SEE BIRDS: Golden Eagles, Prairie Falcons, California Quail, Canyon Wrens, and Western Kingbirds. OTHER INTERESTING BIRDS: White-throated Swifts.

TIPS FOR BIRDING IN CENTRAL OREGON

- Birds can get quiet during warm afternoons, especially in unshaded wildfire sites, so plan to start birding early in the morning.
- Use a gazetteer that shows labeled Forest Service Roads; much of the best birding is far from main roads.
- Before you go, check out the Central Oregon Birders Online e-mail list for current sightings.

- The Oregon Cascades Birding Trail web site has very specific instructions on how to get to lots of sites in the area.
- If you get to Sisters during weekday work hours, stop by the Forest Service office to check out the feeders, scan the list of recently sighted birds, and ask about which burned areas are currently good for viewing woodpeckers.

Ponderosa Pine forest with views of Black Butte and Mount Jefferson

IT TAKES TWO TO TANGO

DANCING AND BREEDING SEASON IN THE KLAMATH BASIN, OREGON

A Red-winged
Blackbird
hitches a ride
on a Sandhill
Crane

HEADQUARTERS:
Klamath Falls

Klamath Falls is situated on Klamath Lake and is close to the Lower Klamath National Wildlife Refuge. The town is large enough to offer a selection of lodging and dining options. Chiloquin to the north is a much smaller town, but the area offers cozy bed and breakfasts and close access to more birding sites.

BEST TIME OF YEAR:
May through July

These months are the best time to enjoy the mating dances, songs, and baby birds of the nesting season. The winter birding here is also amazing and well worth a return trip.

AS WESTERN GREBES perform their synchronized mating dances across the surface of a lake, Yellow-headed Blackbirds bray their raucous songs. The Klamath Basin is perfectly situated where forest meets desert. It is a great place to find a combination of forest, wetland, and open-water birds. You'd need to drive several hours farther east to find similar concentrations of the exciting wetland-nesting birds that live in this area in the summer. Combine that with forest-dwelling woodpeckers and songbirds, and you have enough birding opportunities to keep you busy for a week—but we'll help you condense it all into a weekend.

Klamath Marsh with a view of Mount Scott

PLACES TO GO, FROM NORTH TO SOUTH

Klamath Marsh National Wildlife Refuge

About 60 miles northeast of Klamath Falls, Military Crossing Road (County Road 677) takes you right through the middle of this rich marsh habitat that is alive with birds. Abundant insects provide food for birds in the water, on the cattails, and flying overhead. An evening stop here may be your best chance in Oregon to hear the elusive and rare Yellow Rail. MUST-SEE BIRDS: American Bitterns, Ruddy Ducks, Cinnamon Teals, Yellow-headed Blackbirds, and Common Nighthawks. OTHER INTEREST-ING BIRDS: Soras, Black Terns, and many species of swallow.

Collier State Park in Chiloquin

North of Klamath Falls, this large park contains a mix of conifer forest and riparian habitat along the Williamson River. MUST-SEE BIRDS: Ospreys, White-headed Woodpeckers, American Dippers, Western Tanagers, Black-headed Grosbeaks, Wilson's Warblers, and Belted Kingfishers. OTHER INTERESTING BIRDS: Cliff Swallows and Mountain Chickadees.

Petric Park and Wood River Wetland

These adjacent stops off Highway 62 provide access to a variety of bird habitats. The pond at Petric Park is a good bet for Tricolored Blackbirds. Scan the nearby fields for Sandhill Cranes. The Wood River Wetland offers a raised trail that puts you in the middle of the rich marsh habitat for a view of Agency Lake and restored wetlands. Walk the tree-lined path and you'll hear songbirds calling from every direction. The shallow water on each side of the trail is full of nesting water birds. MUST-SEE BIRDS: Common Nighthawks and Sandhill Cranes. OTHER INTERESTING BIRDS: Tricolored Blackbirds, Bullock's Orioles, Pied-billed Grebes, Willow Flycatchers, and Gadwalls.

Link River Trail

This trail in Klamath Falls is bookended by Moore Park on the north and Veterans Memorial Park on the south. It follows the small Link River but offers views of open water at the parks at either end. MUST-SEE BIRDS: Bonaparte's Gulls, Bald Eagles, American White Pelicans, Western Grebes, and Caspian Terns. OTHER INTERESTING BIRDS: Forster's Terns and Clark's Grebes.

TIPS FOR BIRDING IN THE KLAMATH BASIN

- All these insect-eating birds breed here for a reason. Pack some mosquito repellent in case the insects get too friendly.
- Morning is the best time to watch songbirds, but water birds are active all day long.

Bibliography

Bonar, R. L. 2000. Availability of Pileated Woodpecker cavities and use by other species. *Journal of Wildlife Management* 64: 52–59.

Calkins, J. D. 2007. The family behavior of California Quail: a molecular analysis. *Condor* 109: 962–967.

Cornell Lab of Ornithology and National Audubon Society. eBird web site. http://ebird.org.

Elliott, K. H., J. E. Elliott, L. K. Wilson, I. Jones, and K. Stenerson. 2011. Density-dependence in the survival and reproduction of Bald Eagles: Linkages to chum salmon. *Journal of Wildlife Management* 75: 1688–1699.

Fischer, K. N., R. M. Suryan, D. D. Roby, and G. R. Balogh. 2009. Post-breeding season distribution of Black-footed and Laysan Albatrosses satellite-tagged in Alaska: Inter-specific differences in spatial overlap with North Pacific fisheries. *Biological Conservation* 142: 751–760.

Heinrich, B. 2010. *The Nesting Season: Cuckoos, Cuckolds, and the Invention of Monogamy*. Cambridge, Massachusetts: Harvard University Press.

Jenkins, S. R. 2010. *Post-breeding Habitat Selection by Songbirds in the Headwaters of the Trask River, Northwestern Oregon*. Master's thesis, Oregon State University, Corvallis, Oregon.

Jones, S. L., J. S. Dieni, and A. C. Araya. 2002. Reproductive biology of Canyon Wrens in the Front Range of Colorado. *Wilson Bulletin* 114: 446–449.

Koenig, W. D., D. J. Schaefer, S. Mambelli, and T. E. Dawson. 2008. Acorns, insects, and the diet of adult versus nestling Acorn Woodpeckers. *Journal of Field Ornithology* 79: 280–285.

Kozma, J. M. 2010. Characteristics of trees used by White-headed Woodpeckers for sap feeding in Washington. *Northwestern Naturalist* 91: 81–86.

Marks, J. S., C. S. Crabtree, D. A. Benz, and M. C. Kenne. 2011. Mobbing of Common Nighthawks as cases of mistaken identity. *Wilson Journal of Ornithology* 123: 183–185.

Marshall, D. B., M. G. Hunter, and A. L. Contreras. 2003. *Birds of Oregon: A General Reference*. Corvallis, Oregon: Oregon State University Press.

Martin, T. E., and P. Li. 1992. Life history traits of open- vs. cavity-nesting birds. *Ecology* 73: 579–592.

McNair-Huff, R., and N. McNair-Huff. 2005. *Birding Washington: a Falcon Guide*. Guilford, Connecticut: The Globe Pequot Press.

Muirhead, K. A. 2007. *Marbled Murrelet Foraging Ecology: Spatial and Temporal Characteristics of Habitat Use in Clayoquot Sound, British Columbia*. Master's thesis, University of Victoria, British Columbia.

Newlon, K. R., and V. A. Saab. 2011. Nest-site selection and nest survival of Lewis's Woodpecker in aspen riparian woodlands. *Condor* 113: 183–193.

Opperman, H. 2003. *A Birder's Guide to Washington*. Colorado Springs, Colorado: American Birding Association, Inc.

Poole, A., Ed. Cornell Lab of Ornithology. 2012. The Birds of North America Online. http://bna.birds.cornell.edu/bna.

Rakestraw, J. 2007. *Birding Oregon: a Falcon Guide*. Guilford, Connecticut: The Globe Pequot Press.

Saab, V. A., and K. T. Vierling. 2001. Reproductive success of Lewis's Woodpecker in burned pine and cottonwood riparian forest. *Condor* 105: 491–501.

Seattle Audubon Society. BirdWeb. http://www.birdweb.org.

Shaffer, S. A., Y. Tremblay, H. Weimerskirch, D. Scott, D. R. Thompson, P. M. Sagar, H. Moller, G. A. Taylor, D. G. Foley, B. A. Block, and D. P. Costa. 2006. Migratory shearwaters integrate oceanic resources across the Pacific Ocean in an endless summer. *Proceedings of the National Academy of Sciences* 103: 12799–12802.

Stout, W. E., S. A. Temple, and J. M. Papp. 2006. Landscape correlates of reproductive success for an urban-suburban Red-tailed Hawk population. *Journal of Wildlife Management* 70: 989–997.

Suryan, R. M., D. P. Craig, D. D. Roby, N. D. Chelgren, K. Collis, W. D. Shuford, and D. E. Lyons. 2004. Redistribution and growth of the Caspian Tern population in the Pacific Coast region of North America, 1981–2000. *Condor* 106: 777–790.

Acknowledgments

WRITING OUR FIRST BOOK has reminded us of how much we all rely on help from others. We received an immeasurable amount during the two years we worked on this book: help in the form of information that experts have contributed to books and websites and help in the form of support from our friends, family, and colleagues. Specifically, we now know that we could not have written this book were it not for the following people:

Our teachers, professors, coworkers, and friends who got us hooked on birds and taught us so much about them.

The valuable contributions from proofreaders who generously agreed to read our manuscript and made it the best that it could be. Any remaining errors are ours alone.

The talented photographers whose beautiful work graces this book: Scott Carpenter, Greg Gilson, Jen Sanford, Lois Miller, Jeff Poklen, and Steve Dimock. Had we taken all the photos ourselves, the birds would all have been blurry little dots.

Juree Sondker and all the other folks at Timber Press who helped to shape this book and kept us from accidentally writing a boring textbook. As first-time authors we needed the guidance.

The community of birders who share their knowledge in the field, on listservs, and on eBird.

The Swanson family, who provided enthusiasm, nights at the beach, and beers to celebrate meeting our deadlines.

The Smith and Lacey families, who provided the resources necessary to make a career out of chasing birds.

Karen Munday, who thought of us when asked if she knew anyone who could write a book about birds, and for watering our garden when we left town to scout birding sites.

The Rasmussens, Wellses, and Lyonses, who put us up in their homes during our travels.

The Lonesome Duck Guest Ranch in Chiloquin, Oregon, who gave us a lovely place to stay and provided some great local birding knowledge.

Andie the dog, who is patient when we take her birding and never chases birds.

Our Subaru: Sorry we nearly drove you into the ground while birding all over Oregon and Washington. Thanks for not breaking down.

Index

Photo Credits

SCOTT CARPENTER of Scott Carpenter Photography, pages 4–5, 11, 15, 21, 23, 28, 29, 32, 35, 37, 39, 43, 48, 51, 52, 55, 60, 61, 64, 66, 68–69, 71, 73, 74, 75, 78, 79, 80, 82, 87, 88, 92, 93, 94, 97, 98, 99, 100, 101, 102, 103, 104, 106, 107, 109, 110, 111, 112, 116, 122, 123, 125, 127, 130, 131, 133, 134, 139, 140–141, 144, 146, 152, 154–155, 156, 159, 160, 162, 164, 167, 168, 169, 170, 171, 172, 175, 176, 180, 181, 183, 184, 185, 186, 194–195, 196, 199, 200, 201, 202, 204, 205, 206–207, 211, 215, 220, 221, 224, 227, 230, 233

STEVE DIMOCK of Steve Dimock Photography, page 30

GREG GILSON, pages 20, 27, 36, 45, 46, 47, 56, 58, 84, 90, 148, 178 (left), 190, 192, 217

LOIS MILLER of Lois Miller Fine Art Photography, pages 16–17, 18–19, 24, 38, 40, 42, 44, 62, 76, 120, 129, 142, 188

JEFF POKLEN, page 151

JEN SANFORD, pages 26, 89, 115, 119, 137

All other photos are by the authors.

ABOUT THE AUTHORS

JERRY SWANSON

The authors met in graduate school when they were studying birds in the same lab, and they have been birding together ever since. With their dog, Andie, they split their time between Portland and Pacific City, Oregon.

SARAH SWANSON has worked as an environmental educator for the Audubon Society of Portland. She loves teaching adults and children about natural history by leading field trips and classes.

MAX SMITH is a wildlife biologist currently working with the U.S. Forest Service. Since 2003, he has studied the mechanisms through which invasive plants and wildfire influence the reproductive success of birds.